INTRODUCTION

What is a constitution?

What is a constitution?

RULES OF GOVERNMENT, FREEDOMS AND DUTIES

All organisations need rules to help them work successfully. The rules of a club, for example, will set out the powers and responsibilities of officials such as the secretary or treasurer and indicate how often meetings must be held. They have no effect on what the club does, but without these rules it would not be able to operate.

A country also needs rules of government. This is called a **constitution.** Some of these rules are to do with procedures, such as how a law is made or how often elections must be held. Others are concerned with the amount of power held by the government – specifying what the government can and cannot do. They normally provide an important protection for the rights and freedoms of citizens.

Almost all countries have set out their constitution in a single document. The United Kingdom is one of a small number of countries, including Israel and New Zealand, not to have done this.

Most countries drew up or revised their constitutions after important changes in their history, often when there was a need to set up a new system of government. For example, in 1787 the American Constitution was agreed after settlers there had fought to gain their independence from Britain. The South African constitution was drawn up in 1994 when a new multi-racial government replaced the system of apartheid. Following the overthrow of Saddam Hussein, a new constitution was drawn up by the government of Iraq in 2005.

INSIDE BRITAIN:
A Guide to the UK Constitution

Unlike many other countries, the rules of government in Britain are not set out in a single document. The UK constitution is a mixture of written and unwritten law that has evolved and been adapted over time.

Focusing mainly on England and Wales, this guide tries to explain the rules and procedures by which the UK is governed, and to indicate the extent and the limits of the government's power on everyday life.

dca Department for Constitutional Affairs
Justice, rights and democracy

department for
education and skills
creating opportunity, releasing potential, achieving excellence

The production of this guide has been funded by the DCA and is supported by them and the DfES as part of their shared commitment to improving understanding of justice, rights and democracy within the UK.

cpsu
Commonwealth Policy Studies Unit

The CPSU is a think-tank for the modern Commonwealth, committed to raising awareness of just, accountable governance, the rule of law, and fundamental rights in all member countries.

INDIVIDUALS ENGAGING IN SOCIETY *Citizenship Foundation*

Hodder Murray
www.hoddereducation.co.uk

Caution

In trying to summarise the law, we have had to leave out some details and simplify some of the information. As such, this book should not be taken as proof of legal rights. The law is always developing and changing. To the best of our knowledge we have described the law as it stood on 3rd April 20

CONTENTS

'Inside Britain' has been produced by the Citizenship Foundation, an independent charity, which aims to empower individuals to engage in the wider community through education about the law, democracy and society.

The Citizenship Foundation
63 Gee Street, London EC1V 3RS
Tel 020 7566 4141
Fax 020 7566 4131

www.citizenshipfoundation.org.uk

E-mail:
info@citizenshipfoundation.org.uk

Charity Reg. No. 801360

EG39260

Authors Tony Thorpe and Richard Jarvis

Concept devised by Richard Bourne, Commonwealth Policy Studies Unit, Institute of Commonwealth Studies

We would like to thank the following for their help in preparing this guide: Mark Askam, Rocio Ferro, Rebecca Galbraith, Mike Gibas, Robert Hazell, Fiona Hogarth, Janany Kathirgamanathan, Dan Mace, Lizzie Macey, Emran Mian, Lena Whitaker, Adam Williams and in particular, members of the steering group, Richard Bourne, Tony Breslin, Andrew Holden, Ted Huddleston, John Lloyd, Shula Maibaum, Jan Newton, Don Rowe, and Judith Simpson and students and teachers from Bishop David Brown School, Woking; Kingston College, Kingston; St Michael's RC School, Billingham; Skinners School, Tunbridge Wells; Thorpe St Andrew School, Norwich; Whalley Range High School, Manchester.

The Publishers would like to thank the following for permission to reproduce copyright material:
Photo credits: All images from iStockphoto.com except: Ablestock.com Cover, p5, 17, 21, 30, 33, 61 ,63, 67, 81, 99, 108, 109, 115, 121, 122, 139; British Board of Film Classification © ™ p37; Citizenship Foundation p8; Corbis p89, 92 © Sean Sexton Collection, 96 © Geray Sweeney, 145; Corel p60; Council of Europe/Richard Rogers Partnership p136; Digital Vision p29; EMPICS 80, 90; Eyewire p12-70, 53, 114; House of Commons p122; The Illustrated London News Royalty Free Images p22, 127; Imperial War Museum, London p36; Ingram Publishing p41; National Portrait Gallery p39; Nomad p49, 63, 64, 99, 122, 128, 134, 137, 141; Palace of Westminster Collection 86, 123, 131; Parliamentary Recording Unit p119; Photodisc p28, 37, 74, 79, 112; © Terry Moore p132, 133; Welwyn Hatfield Council p103.

Every effort has been made to trace all copyright holders, but if any have been inadvertently overlooked the Publishers will be pleased to make the necessary arrangements at the first opportunity.

Although every effort has been made to ensure that website addresses are correct at time of going to press, Hodder Murray cannot be held responsible for the content of any website mentioned in this book. It is sometimes possible to find a relocated web page by typing in the address of the home page for a website in the URL window of your browser.

Hodder Headline's policy is to use papers that are natural, renewable and recyclable products and made from wood grown in sustainable forests. The logging and manufacturing processes are expected to conform to the environmental regulations of the country of origin.

Orders: please contact Bookpoint Ltd, 130 Milton Park, Abingdon, Oxon OX14 4SB. Telephone: (44) 01235 827720. Fax: (44) 01235 400454. Lines are open 9.00 – 5.00, Monday to Saturday, with a 24-hour message answering service. Visit our website at www.hoddereducation.co.uk

© The Citizenship Foundation 2006
First published in 2006 by Hodder Murray, an Imprint of Hodder Education,
a member of the Hodder Headline Group,
338 Euston Road, London NW1 3BH

Impression number   5 4 3 2 1
Year   2010 2009 2008 2007 2006

Designed in England by Nomad Graphique
Printed in Italy.

A catalogue record for this title is available from the British Library

ISBN-10: 0 340 92986 3
ISBN-13: 978 0340 929 865

The British constitution

Unwritten?

The history of Britain has been one of gradual change, rather than great upheaval. As a result, the British constitution has evolved over many years. Instead of being set down in one formal document, the rules for governing Britain are to be found in many different places. Our constitution is to be found in customs, **conventions** and laws.

Conventions

Much of the British constitution is based on unwritten customs and rules, called conventions. These are a fundamental part of our constitution even though they cannot be enforced as rules of law.

Conventions develop gradually to become accepted practice, and many are unwritten. For example, it was never formally stated that the queen or king must agree to any proposal for a new law passed by both Houses of **Parliament**. However, since 1707, no king or queen has refused to do this, and so it has now become a convention that he or she should always give their assent. A more recent convention is that the king or queen is required to appoint as Prime Minister the leader of the majority party in the House of Commons.

Constitutional conventions do not last for ever. People simply stop observing them when they are no longer needed. For example, it used to be a convention that a government minister had to be present at a royal birth to make sure that the heir to the throne was not an impostor.

Because unwritten conventions are such an important part of the UK constitution it is often said that ours is an 'unwritten' constitution. However many of the rules are to be found in a variety of written documents.

What is a constitution?

Laws

The *Magna Carta*, signed in 1215, is one of the oldest written documents that has shaped the UK constitution. Another is the *Bill of Rights 1689*, parts of which are still in force today. Examples of more recent laws of constitutional importance passed by Parliament include those that brought Britain into the European Community in 1972, established the Scottish Parliament in 1998 and the *Human Rights Act 1998*.

Law is also created by judges as a result of the decisions they reach in cases that they hear in court. This is known as **common law** and some of these decisions determine the powers of government and the rights and freedoms of citizens.

Not above the law

In 1994, 'M', a teacher and citizen of Zaire (now the Democratic Republic of Congo), claimed political asylum In the UK. However, hls application was turned down by the Home Office, who ordered his removal from Britain.

M's solicitor appealed against this decision, but his case was not heard until M was already on the plane back to Zaire. The judge said that he needed more time to consider the evidence and ordered M's immediate return to Britain. The Home Secretary, however, overruled the judge and ordered that M should continue his journey.

The Home Secretary's decision was challenged in court. The case reached the Law Lords – the UK's highest court – who decided that, by ignoring the judge's order, the Home Secretary had committed an offence.

Flexible

Changing the constitution, in those countries with a written constitution, requires a special procedure. Often there is a Supreme or Constitutional Court to carry this out.

Although there are laws in the UK that are regarded as part of the constitution, they have no special importance in our system. In the UK, Parliament is supreme, and may make or change any law (including those affecting the constitution) that it wishes. As a result, the UK constitution is considered to be flexible and able to adapt to changing circumstances. In 1996 it was possible for Parliament to pass a new law very quickly to outlaw handguns, following the shooting of 16 primary school children and their teacher in the Scottish town of Dunblane. This could not have been done so quickly in the United States, for example, where the right to carry handguns is part of the written constitution.

Separation of powers

Many constitutions try to make sure that the government does not have too much power. This is done by separating the powers of government into three branches. The shorthand names for these are the **legislature**, the **executive**, and the **judiciary**. The reason for this separation is to prevent too much power from becoming concentrated in the hands of one person or one institution.

Written constitutions, drafted at a single point in a nation's history, are able to include clear rules that separate the powers of the different branches of government. In the US, for example, the President (the executive) has no power over the affairs of Congress (the legislature) or the Supreme Court (the judiciary).

The separation of powers in the UK is not as clear-cut as it is in countries with written constitutions. For example, the Prime Minister and government ministers in Britain have considerable influence over laws passed by Parliament. This is because they are also Members of Parliament and from the largest party of government.

Three branches of government

THE EXECUTIVE

- Proposing the law
- Government
- The Prime Minister, government ministers

THE LEGISLATURE

- Making the law
- Parliament
- Members of Parliament in the House of Commons and peers in the House of Lords

THE JUDICIARY

- Applying the law
- Courts
- Judges

Freedoms and duties

The UK constitution also gives citizens and the **state** certain freedoms and duties. Traditionally, British citizens have the freedom to act as they wish, unless they are prevented from doing so by a particular law or laws. They have also had duties to the state – such as serving on a jury, giving evidence in court and at certain times serving in the armed forces.

Human Rights

Constitutions in many countries include a section on **human rights** – sometimes added separately. Until recently, the human rights of citizens of the UK had not been guaranteed by any part of the constitution, although many were available under common and **statute** law.

However, the *Human Rights Act 1998*, which came into force in 2000, incorporates into UK law nearly all the rights contained in the European Convention on Human Rights, see page 110. These include rights to a fair trial, freedom of expression and peaceful assembly. Few of these rights are absolute, in that they may be limited or withdrawn under certain circumstances. Changes of this kind indicate how the UK constitution is constantly evolving.

What is a constitution?

The words we use

Most of the technical terms used in this guide are explained as they are introduced. The following words are used throughout the text.

Act of Parliament
A law that has been passed by Parliament and received the royal assent. It is also called a statute.

Constitution
The laws, rules and customs that set out the ways in which a country should be governed and the rights and duties of the state and its citizens.

Common law
Law that has been made by judges. It began to develop in the twelfth century when judges travelled the country providing justice and sorting out disputes. Their decisions were written down and then applied to cases where the facts were similar. Cases were judged by common standards, and this became known as common law. It is still being applied and developed by courts today.

Convention
Unwritten customs and rules.

Executive
This is the group that has the job of governing the country. It is headed by the Prime Minister and Cabinet, but also includes, in practice, the Civil Service and local government. Britain's membership of the European Union means that the executive also includes other European institutions, such as the European Commission which is responsible for, among other things, making sure EU laws and treaties are being properly applied.

Human rights
Basic rights and freedoms, to which everyone is entitled, that are designed to limit the power of the state. Human rights include the right to a fair trial, freedom of speech, thought and conscience, and freedom from torture and slavery.

Judiciary
The system of courts and judges.

Legislature
The body of people with the power to make and change the law. In the UK, this is Parliament.

Magna Carta
The *Magna Carta* was an agreement, drawn up in 1215, between King John and his barons, in which the King dealt with a number of their grievances. The charter sets out certain rights that the King agreed to respect; these include freedom from exorbitant taxes, access to justice and the right to a fair trial. The *Magna Carta* is of great historical importance, but few parts remain on the statute book today.

Parliament
Parliament, consisting of the House of Commons and the House of Lords, is with the Crown, the law-making body of the UK.

State
In general terms, a country or community with its own government. The word is also used, however, to describe the general system of authority in a country made up of the government and all the other institutions through which people are ordered and controlled.

Statute
A law passed by Parliament. Another name for an Act of Parliament.

THE INDIVIDUAL AND THE STATE

Life & liberty

PROTECTING PEOPLE'S LIVES

One of the most important duties of the state is the protection of its citizens' lives. All states that have signed the European Convention on Human Rights (see page 110) must have laws that protect human life and allow the taking of life in only the most exceptional circumstances.

People cannot be ill-treated or tortured by the state, nor should they suffer harmful state intrusion or disruption of their lives.

Whilst most people welcome a safe and secure society, there are important questions about how this should be achieved and about the kinds of powers that should be available to the police.

> The European Convention on Human Rights, Article 2
>
> "Everyone's life shall be protected by law. No one shall be deprived of his life intentionally, save in the execution of a sentence of a court following his conviction of a crime for which this penalty is provided by law."

The right to life

Human life has been protected by law in Britain for more than a thousand years. There are records as far back as the seventh century listing the penalties for murder.

Today, the state has a duty to take all reasonable measures to safeguard citizens' lives. This is guaranteed by the *Human Rights Act 1998*, which brought the European Convention on Human Rights into UK law, see page 110.

Unlawful killing

Murder – that is unlawful and deliberate killing – is a long-established offence. However, killing another human being under certain circumstances *may* be tolerated.

Self-defence

If a person kills someone who is threatening or attacking them, they may be able to claim that they acted in self-defence. This will be acceptable in law only if it can be shown that they used no more force than was absolutely necessary.

In a similar way, the police or security forces may very occasionally kill someone either unintentionally, or whom they believe is about to commit a serious violent offence. When dealing with cases of this kind, a court will try to decide whether the officer acted in a reasonable and justifiable way in the situation they faced at the time. A question often asked in these circumstances is whether the action by the officer was in proportion to the risks or dangers involved.

Enquiry

As well as protecting its citizens from unlawful killing, the state also has a duty to investigate violent deaths.

Death in custody

In 2000, Zahid Mubarek, aged 19, was sentenced to 90 days in a young offenders' institution for car crime and theft. Towards the end of his sentence he was placed in the same cell as 20-year-old Robert Stewart, who was being held for sending racist hate mail and was known to be dangerous and disturbed. On the day before he was due to be released, Zahid Mubarek was battered to death by his cell mate.

Although Robert Stewart was sentenced to life imprisonment for this crime, Zahid Mubarek's family believed that there should have been a public enquiry into the killing, and took their case to court. The High Court judge agreed, but his decision was overruled by the Court of Appeal. Finally, the family applied to the House of Lords. The Law Lords decided that the government had been wrong to refuse an enquiry. They said that the state had a duty, under Article 2 (see page 12) to investigate the death, particularly because the person concerned was in custody at the time.

The death penalty

The death penalty for murder was abolished in Britain in 1965. In 1998, under the *Crime and Disorder Act*, the removal of the death penalty was extended to cover all crimes committed in peacetime, including treason and piracy. The last executions in Britain took place in August 1964.

Life & liberty

Torture

Torture is the deliberate infliction of extreme mental or physical suffering, usually in an effort to obtain information or a confession. It has been prohibited by law in England for almost 400 years and the prohibition of torture is one of the strongest rights under the European Convention.

> The European Convention on Human Rights, Article 3
>
> "No one shall be subjected to torture or to inhuman or degrading treatment or punishment."

This ban also extends to information obtained by torture conducted by other states. In 2005, the Law Lords ruled that Britain could not use information obtained by torture by officials in other countries against terror suspects in Britain.

Unlawful

In 1978, the European Court of Human Rights decided that methods used by the British in interrogating terrorist suspects in Northern Ireland broke Article 3 of the Convention. These techniques, which included sleep, food and drink deprivation, and subjecting suspects to loud noises for extended periods, were judged to be completely unacceptable.

A right to life?

Abortion

In the past, judges at the European Court of Human Rights have been called on to decide whether the ban on depriving someone of their life applies to the unborn child.

In answer, the Court has ruled that a foetus is not a human being, and that, therefore, the protection of the law does not extend to the unborn.

Complex and sensitive

Shortly after they had separated, a man learned that his wife was pregnant and intended to have an abortion. He tried to obtain a court order to stop this, claiming, amongst other things, that having an abortion would break Article 2, 'The right to life'.

By the time the application reached the European Court of Human Rights, the abortion had already taken place, but the judges decided to continue with the case as it covered an important point of law. They decided that a right to life could apply only to those who have already been born and noted that the law on abortion varies from one European state to another. The judges decided that they were not prepared to choose one country's law above those of others and therefore ruled that, under the European Convention, abortion was not a breach of the right to life.

The right to die

Although committing suicide ceased to be a criminal offence in Britain in 1961, it remains a crime to help or encourage someone else to take their own life.

Assisted suicide

In 2002 Diane Pretty was suffering from a terminal illness. She wanted her husband to help her end her life – something that she could not do herself. He was willing to do this, but the authorities would not guarantee that he would not face prosecution for helping in her suicide.

Diane Pretty tried to have this ruling overturned and took her case to the European Court of Human Rights. She claimed that her right to life also gave her the right to choose her manner of death. The Court disagreed, stating that the state's duty to protect life could not be seen as giving someone the right "to choose death rather than life". Soon after the case, Diane Pretty died, after experiencing breathing difficulties for ten days.

However, a doctor will respect the wishes of a mentally competent adult who either states, or expresses in writing in advance, their wish not to receive life-sustaining treatment.

In addition, courts have allowed doctors to stop giving treatment or withdraw food and water from patients who are in a 'persistent vegetative state' when both the doctors and the patients' relatives believe that it is no longer in the best interest of the patient to continue to receive treatment.

Life & liberty

▶ The quality of life

Although the state can't protect individuals from difficulty and tragedy, it does have a duty not to interfere with, or to take action that damages, the quality of people's private lives. It also has a duty not to interfere with very personal aspects of people's lives.

Any interference by the state in these matters must be in accordance with the law and necessary for reasons of national security, public safety, or for the protection of others.

Cases involving the right to respect for private and family life cover all kinds of situations. For example, a disabled couple from London successfully challenged their local housing department, under Article 8, over the council's

> The European Convention on Human Rights, Article 8
>
> "Everyone has the right to respect for his private and family life, his home and his correspondence."

repeated failure to provide the couple with appropriate help and support. This left them both, and their children, living in what were described in court as "humiliating conditions".

Discrimination against people because of their sexual orientation has also been challenged under Article 8. As a result, the age of consent is the same for gay and heterosexual couples, and gay members of the armed forces cannot be dismissed for their sexuality.

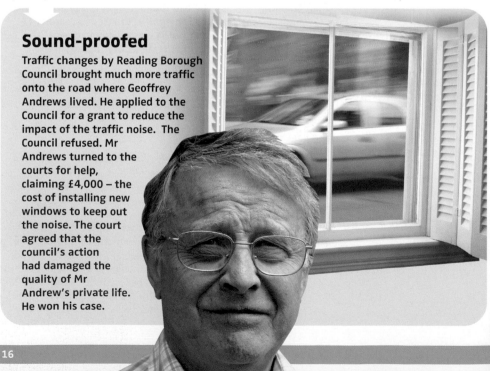

Sound-proofed

Traffic changes by Reading Borough Council brought much more traffic onto the road where Geoffrey Andrews lived. He applied to the Council for a grant to reduce the impact of the traffic noise. The Council refused. Mr Andrews turned to the courts for help, claiming £4,000 – the cost of installing new windows to keep out the noise. The court agreed that the council's action had damaged the quality of Mr Andrew's private life. He won his case.

Liberty

It is important for the government of any country to be able to maintain law and order and to prevent and detect crime. In order to do this the police are given powers to stop and question people, and when necessary, to take away their liberty.

The powers of the police are set out in common law (see page 135) and in a number of Acts of Parliament. The Act that probably applies to most situations in which the police deal with the public is the *Police and Criminal Evidence Act 1984*.

The protection of liberty is a key part of the European Convention on Human Rights. Several of the Articles are designed to prevent an abuse of power by the state in excessively limiting citizens' liberty.

> The European Convention on Human Rights, Article 5
>
> "Everyone has the right to liberty and security of person."

Police powers

Generally speaking, the police do not have the power to stop and detain members of the public without a valid reason. It is not acceptable, for example, for an officer to stop and question someone simply because of that person's skin colour, dress, or hairstyle – or because they have been in trouble before.

Helping the police with their enquiries

The police could not do their job without help from the public. But, as a *general* rule, no one can be required to help the police or give the police information – unless it specifically says so in law. It is an offence, however, to lie to the police, to give false information, or to waste police time.

One group of people who *must* help the police are drivers of road vehicles, who are required by law when asked to give an officer the name and address of the owner of the vehicle. Refusing to do so is an offence.

If a person is asked to go to a police station voluntarily to help the police with their enquiries, they may refuse. If, however, the police then decide to arrest them, they have no choice and must attend.

Refusing to answer questions

The right of the accused to remain silent is a long-established principle in British law. It protects suspects from incriminating themselves under the pressure of questioning.

A right to silence also upholds the other traditional principle that a person accused of a crime is innocent, until proved guilty. It is the job of the prosecution in court to *prove* that the accused is guilty. There is no requirement for the defendant to prove their innocence.

Life & liberty

Until relatively recently, a suspect's refusal to answer questions could not generally be commented on at their trial. Today, refusal to answer questions, either at the police station or in court, may be used as evidence against the accused. The judge may invite the jury to draw their own conclusions from the silence of a defendant. However, this cannot be the only evidence against the accused for them to be found guilty.

Arrest

Police officers may arrest anyone whom they believe is about to commit, or has already committed, an offence. This now includes minor offences, such as dropping litter.

Police officers do not have the power to search or to hold people to check whether there are any grounds for arrest.

Procedure   The law requires that arrests are carried out in a particular way. This means that the police should use only reasonable force to make the arrest and should inform the suspect as soon as possible that they have been arrested, and the reason for this.

A person arrested is also entitled to see a solicitor, to have someone told where they are, and to have a copy of the *Codes of Practice*, which explain the procedures the police should follow when questioning suspects.

Unlawful arrest   There are two things that people can do who believe that they have been arrested and held without a proper reason.

The first is to apply for *habeas corpus*. This is a Latin phrase meaning "you must have the body". Its origins are thought to go back to a time before the *Magna Carta* when it was used by the king to bring a prisoner to court to testify at a trial. By the time it became an Act

of Parliament in 1679, it had become a way of establishing the legality of someone's detention.

Although it is rarely used today, anyone who believes that they have been unlawfully detained may issue a writ (or order) requiring them to be brought before a judge who will decide whether the detention is lawful.

Secondly, a person who is wrongly arrested may also be able to sue for damages, and will need to show that the police did not have a good enough reason to make the arrest.

Fowl play

Twelve ramblers feeding ducks and swans at a lake near Abergavenny were arrested by police in order to prevent a breach of the peace and to ensure that a local hunt passed off without protest. The walkers were driven to the police station in Brecon, where they were held there for more than five hours.

The ramblers said they had no intention of disrupting the hunt. They sued the police for wrongful arrest and each obtained £2,000 in compensation.

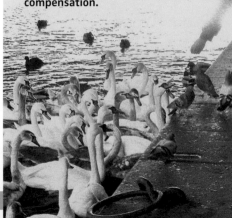

Detention

A person cannot normally be held by the police for more than 24 hours without being charged, but if a serious offence is being investigated, this period may be extended to 96 hours (four days) with the approval of a magistrates' court.

Terrorist offences Further legislation deals with people held in connection with terrorist offences. In response to the London bombings of July 2005, the *Terrorism Act 2006* extends the maximum period for which these suspects can be held without charge from 14 to 28 days.

If the terrorist suspect is from overseas and cannot be deported back to their own country, the Home Secretary may, under the *Anti-Terrorism and Security Act 2001*, order their indefinite detention in the UK without trial. This is largely because international law states that a person may not be compulsorily deported where there is a risk that they may be tortured or sentenced to death.

Questioning by the police

In almost every case, any suspect interviewed by the police has the right to receive advice from a solicitor and to have a solicitor present at the interview. This right may be withheld only in very serious cases when the police believe that access to a solicitor might damage the investigation, or endanger or alert other people.

Children and young people under 17 should not normally be interviewed without a parent or other responsible adult present. There are also rules governing the way in which witnesses and suspects should be treated. For example, the police should not use force or pressure to obtain answers to questions, nor should they directly threaten someone who, for example, is refusing to make a statement.

Fingerprints, photographs and samples

The police are entitled to take fingerprints, photographs and non-intimate DNA samples from anyone they arrest, with or without that person's consent.

If a suspect refuses to give a blood or urine sample, the court will be told of this if the case later goes to trial.

Complaints against the police

A person who feels that they have witnessed or suffered police misconduct may make an official complaint. This may be made by them, through a friend or solicitor, or through an organisation like the Citizens Advice Bureau. The complaint can be made at a police station, or to the Independent Police Complaints Commission.

If a person is unhappy about the way in which their complaint has been dealt with, they have the right under the *Police Reform Act 2002* to lodge an appeal.

Meetings, groups & marches

FREEDOM TO GATHER, TALK AND MEET

It is a long-established right that people in Britain have the freedom to gather together, to talk to and to meet whoever they like – as long as they don't break any existing law in doing so.

These freedoms have existed under common law for more than 700 years. They also became guaranteed by an Act of Parliament in 1998 when the *Human Rights Act* brought the **European Convention on Human Rights** into UK law.

There are some circumstances, however, when these freedoms may be limited or taken away. This is likely to be for reasons of public safety, national security, or to protect the rights of others.

The European Convention on Human Rights, Article 11

"Everyone has the right to freedom of peaceful assembly and to freedom of association with others, including the right to form and join trade unions …

"No restrictions shall be placed on these rights other than … are prescribed by law and … are in the interest of national security or public safety …"

Freedom of movement

A right of way

Everyone has a general right to walk along a public footpath, bridleway, byway, or road – known as public rights of way. A person may stop and admire the view, as long as they do not cause an obstruction.

There are, however, certain restrictions. It is against the law, for example, to walk along the side of a motorway or use certain types of vehicles in certain areas. Bicycles, for example, may not be used on motorways, footpaths, or on the pavement.

Trespass

All land in Britain is owned by someone. These might be private individuals, local authorities, government departments, or the Crown, see page 91. Anyone who goes onto land to which they are not allowed access, or against the wishes of the landowner, becomes a trespasser – and can be required to leave by the owner.

Open country

Today, under the *Countryside and Rights of Way Act 2000*, people have a legal right of access on foot to many more parts of the country than they did in the past. This right, however, only applies to open uncultivated land – and not to someone's back garden or to fields where a farmer has planted crops.

Travel in Europe

Citizens of EU member states have the right to travel to and around any EU country they wish, as long as they have a valid passport or identity card. This right may be restricted only for reasons of public order, public security, or public health.

Meetings, groups & marches

▶ Trade unions and political organisations

Trade unions

Almost everyone is free to join (or not join) a trade union. Only members of the armed forces, the police and certain public officials may not belong to one.

Not all employers want to work with unions. But, in organisations with more than 20 employees, unions may be able to require the employer to negotiate with them.

No Contract! No Peace!
UNITE HERE!

Union membership, however, has not always been allowed in Britain. Throughout the early nineteenth century, until 1824, it was illegal for workers to organise together for higher wages or shorter working hours. Those found breaking the law faced two months' hard labour, or three months in prison. Even after trade unions became legal, workers were still likely to face penalties for trying to form some kind of association.

The Tolpuddle Martyrs

During the 1830s, many farm workers in England lived in great poverty. Wages were very low and they had no land on which to grow crops and graze animals. When George Loveless, a farm worker from the village of Tolpuddle in Dorset, asked his employer for a wage rise – his pay was lowered, from nine to six shillings a week.

Knowing that it was impossible to live on so little, Loveless and some of the other workers decided to form a farm labourer's society or union, and in doing so, swore each other to secrecy. But word of their action spread and, within two months, posters were put up in the village warning that anyone joining a trade union would be punished. Three days after the notices appeared, George Loveless and five other members of his union were arrested.

As trade unions were no longer illegal, the men were instead charged with making an illegal oath, under the *Illegal Oaths Act 1797*, a law originally designed to discourage mutiny in the navy. Their trial was unfair, from beginning to end. Several of the jury were amongst those who had brought the original charges against the farm workers. George Loveless and the five other union members were found guilty and sentenced to seven years' transportation to Australia.

Industrial action

In the early 1980s the government passed a number of laws designed to limit trade union activity and industrial action. This was a reaction to Britain's reputation at the time as a country held back through strikes and low productivity.

The right to picket – that is to protest outside a building or factory in order to dissuade people from entering – was restricted, and it became unlawful for workers to strike "in sympathy" with others involved in an industrial dispute. Trade unions were required to ballot their members before taking industrial action and employers were given the right to apply for a court order, preventing unions from strike action.

Although the government of Britain has changed several times since these laws were passed, almost all are still in place.

No unions allowed

GCHQ, based in Cheltenham, Gloucestershire, is the Government Communication Headquarters and employs more than 4,000 staff. Their job is to provide intelligence information for the government and to work closely with organisations like MI5 and MI6.

In 1984 the government withdrew the right of civil servants working for GCHQ to belong to a trade union (which they had had since 1946), fearing that industrial action by GCHQ workers would endanger national security. Most of the GCHQ staff eventually accepted this decision. However, a small group of workers applied to the European Commission of Human Rights, claiming that the removal of their union rights broke Article 11 of the European Convention.

The Commission decided that the ban on union membership did break the first part of Article 11, but agreed with the government's claim that, for reasons of national security, it should be allowed. Fourteen employees, who would not give up their union membership, were dismissed.

In 1997, a new government came to power, announcing that the restriction on union membership would be removed. In September 1997, the first of the fourteen GCHQ employees who had been dismissed returned to work.

Meetings, groups & marches

Political parties

Almost everyone is free to join a political party, to stand for election or to canvas for their party. However, this right is not available to people who work in certain sections of the civil service and local government. Members of the police are barred from taking an active role in politics.

Although people are allowed to belong to almost any political group, it is an offence, under the *Public Order Act 1936*, to wear a uniform signifying an association with a political organisation in any public place or at a public meeting.

The Cable Street riots

The ban on wearing political uniforms in public stems from the violent clashes between supporters of the British Union of Fascists and those of the political left in London during the 1930s.

The fascists, led by Sir Oswald Mosley, blamed Jewish immigrants for much of the poverty and unemployment facing the country at the time. Huge parades were organised by fascists, who marched in their black para-military style uniforms, through areas where Jewish people had settled. These situations often became very violent.

One of the biggest clashes took place in Cable Street in the East End of London in 1936 when anti-fascists broke up a large Blackshirt parade, led by Mosley. There was fierce fighting as the left-wing demonstrators tried to stop the parade and police did their best to allow the march to continue. Eventually the police ordered the parade to turn round to prevent further bloodshed. Shortly after this the *Public Order Act* was passed, giving the police much more power to control demonstrations – and outlawing, in England and Wales, paramilitary-style demonstrations.

Terrorism

In recent years, the government has made membership of certain terrorist groups illegal in the UK.

Under the *Terrorism Act 2000*, 25 international organisations are banned in the UK. These include groups such as Al Qaida, believed to be responsible for the 9/11 attacks in the United States. Membership of 14 Irish groups, such as the Irish Republican Army and the Ulster Volunteer Force, is also forbidden.

Under the *Terrorism Act*, it is an offence to belong to (or to claim to belong to) a banned organisation, or to take part in activities which support that organisation.

Assemblies and gatherings

Although people can generally meet and gather where they wish, there are some circumstances in which this may be stopped by the police or a court.

Public meetings may be banned if they are likely to:
- **cause a breach of the peace, ie unnecessary disturbance**
- **prevent the police from carrying out their duty**
- **block the road or path.**

In such cases, the police and courts have to decide whether the threat to public order or the disruption of traffic outweighs the right of people to meet or demonstrate.

Turned back

In 1985, during the Miners' Strike, the police stopped a car carrying four miners. The police suspected that the men were on their way to another pit to join the picket line in support of other miners, and believed that this might cause a breach of the peace. The miners were ordered to turn back. They refused, and were arrested.

In court, the judge said that it was not unreasonable for the police to believe that there was a risk of a breach of the peace if the miners had been allowed to continue their journey. He decided that the police had not broken the law by preventing them from doing so.

Meetings, groups & marches

Meetings

The police can enter a public meeting if they believe it is likely to become disorderly, but have no right to enter private meetings (meetings open by invitation only) unless the organisers invite them to do so.

Many meeting places, such as school halls, are owned by the local authority, and a local authority is quite entitled not to allow its premises to be used by organisations of which it disapproves.

One exception to this, however, is during elections when all candidates are entitled to hold campaign meetings in local school halls or other public buildings.

Disruption

It is an offence under the *Public Meetings Act 1908* to try to break up a lawful public meeting by behaving in a disorderly way, or by trying to get others to do so. If this occurs, the chair of the meeting may call the police.

Not welcome

Many Liverpool parents and teachers were shocked to hear that BNP leader Nick Griffin was due to speak at a local school during the 2003 local election. The council spokesman stated: "Under the *Representation of the People Act*, all candidates have the right to use council premises, including schools, for election meetings."

Although the council could not ban the meeting, they did require the BNP to take out sufficient insurance to cover possible damage. The party was unable to do this, and the booking was cancelled.

Marches and demonstrations

Under the *Public Order Act 1986*, anyone wishing to organise a march or procession that is designed to express a particular view or commemorate an event, must notify the police (at the nearest police station) at least seven days before it is due to take place. The law applies to processions of any size including, for example, a small group of people protesting about the closure of a local park. Failing to give notice of a procession is an offence, with a fine of up to £1,000.

If the police feel that the march is likely to cause serious damage to property or seriously disrupt the life of the community, they may require the organisers to follow certain conditions over the timing or route of the march. If there is no way of preventing serious public disorder, the procession may be banned.

Under the *Serious Organised Crime and Police Act 2005*, there is a small area in London, within a half-mile radius of the Houses of Parliament, where assemblies and demonstrations are forbidden – unless they have been cleared by the police.

Public assemblies

People have a general freedom to gather on private property or public land – although it is a trespass to do so on private land without permission of the landowner. Assemblies on public land are controlled by local by-laws and an offence is committed if these are broken.

If the police believe that an assembly or gathering is likely to cause serious damage to property or life in the local community, they have the power to ban the assembly and to turn people away within a five-mile radius.

Raves
Under the *Criminal Justice and Public Order Act 1994*, police have the power to order people to leave any gathering of 20 or more people, if they believe the noise of the music is likely to cause serious distress to local people. If the organisers fail to follow police instructions, their sound equipment and vehicles etc may be seized.

Picketing
Picketing takes place when a group of people gather together outside a building to make a protest or to try to persuade others from entering. This might be connected with an industrial dispute, or some kind of consumer or political action.

Generally speaking people are free to picket peacefully, as long as they don't cause an obstruction or behave in a way that threatens or intimidates others.

Speech & expression

A LONG TRADITION

In Britain, there is a long tradition of freedom of speech and expression – and this has included the right to criticise the government in public in the strongest of ways. However, there are limits on what people may say, write, publish or broadcast, and these are set out in statute and common law.

Today, freedom of expression in Britain is also protected by the *Human Rights Act 1998*, which brought the European Convention on Human Rights into UK law. However, freedom of expression is not an absolute right and may, for various reasons, be restricted.

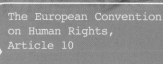

> The European Convention on Human Rights, Article 10
>
> "Everyone has the right to freedom of expression. This right shall include freedom to hold opinions and to receive and impart information and ideas without interference by public authority …"
>
> "… these freedoms … may be subject to … restrictions … in the interests of national security … or public safety, for the prevention of disorder or crime, for the protection of health or morals, for the protection of the reputation or rights of others, for preventing the disclosure of information received in confidence, or for maintaining the authority and impartiality of the judiciary."

Limits to freedom of speech and expression

The importance of free speech

The freedom to say or write what we like, however critical we are of others, is an important part of democratic society.

Without freedom of speech, there can be no debate or discussion about important issues of the day; nor can people express their disagreement over a government's actions or policies.

However, although the right of people to say and publish what they like is protected in law, it is limited by the right of others to prevent the publication of offensive or damaging remarks, and to obtain compensation for damage caused to their reputation.

Defamation

Attacking and damaging a person's reputation is known in law as defamation. If it is spoken it is *slander*. If it is written or broadcast it is *libel*.

A person who believes that their reputation has been damaged, or that they have been shunned or ridiculed as a result of a false statement, may seek compensation through the courts.

Not true

A woman who was a witness in a murder trial found herself accused by *The Sun* of helping the murderers go on the run. In court, lawyers for *The Sun* accepted that the story was wrong and apologised for the distress caused. The woman was awarded a substantial sum in damages.

A statement is defamatory in law only if it is heard or read by other people. It is not defamatory to call someone a thief if there is no one else present to hear the conversation.

Individuals and companies can sue for slander or libel – but governments and local authorities cannot. In 1993, an article appeared in the *Sunday Times* accusing Derbyshire County Council of certain improper financial practices. The Council brought an action for libel against the paper, but the courts decided that the case could not go ahead. The judges felt that it was important for government bodies (like local councils) to be open to public criticism – and that the right to criticise such groups should not be restricted.

Speech & expression

Members of Parliament

Members of both the House of Commons and the House of Lords have a special right to freedom of speech. This is known as a parliamentary privilege, and allows MPs and Lords to debate freely, without the risk of being arrested or sued for what they might say.

Parliamentary privilege dates back to the times when Parliament was trying to establish its independence, and become free from interference by the king or queen. This particular right, set out in Article IX of the *Bill of Rights 1689*, states "speeches and debates ... in Parliament ought not to be impeached or questioned in any other court or place outside of Parliament".

Racial hatred

Freedom of speech and expression may be limited in order to protect people from harmful and hurtful statements about their colour, nationality or ethnic group.

Under the *Public Order Act 1986*, it is an offence to stir up racial hatred by using threatening or insulting words or by displaying threatening or abusive material. In a similar way, shouting racial abuse at football matches is also a criminal offence under the *Football (Offences) Act 1991*.

Threatening and abusive material

A man who put leaflets through the doors of hundreds of homes in Glasgow, alleging that attacks had been made on people in the area by Muslim youths, was found guilty of inciting racial hatred, and sentenced to four months' imprisonment. The court decided that the information in the leaflet was inaccurate and that there was no threat of violence against white members of the community, as the leaflet claimed.

Banned

Three Blackburn Rovers fans were fined a total of £1,200 and banned from attending football matches for five years after being found guilty of racially abusing Birmingham City player, Dwight Yorke. As the black player warmed up on the sidelines, the three men made monkey gestures and shouted racial abuse.

Blasphemy

Under the law of blasphemy in Britain, it is an offence, punishable by imprisonment, to say or to publish something that causes outrage to the feelings of members of the Anglican faith, or denies the truth of the Bible or the Book of Common Prayer. There is no similar protection in law for other Christian denominations (such as Catholics and Methodists) or for other religions. There have been calls either to widen the law to include these groups, or to abolish it completely.

In 1991, a group of British Muslims tried to have Salman Rushdie, author of *The Satanic Verses*, charged with blasphemy, claiming statements in the book were grossly offensive to Muslims. The court decided that a summons could not be issued against Mr Rushdie as the blasphemy law is only concerned with the Anglican faith.

Prosecution

John Gott was the last person in England to be sent to prison for blasphemy in 1921, sentenced to nine months' hard labour. His offence was writing a pamphlet comparing Jesus Christ to a circus clown.

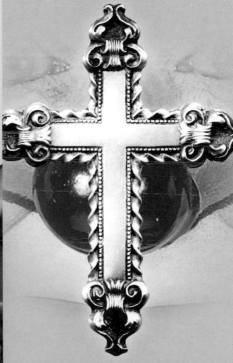

The last successful prosecution in England for blasphemy was in 1978 when the publisher of *Gay News* published a poem and illustration suggesting that Jesus Christ had been homosexual. Originally sentenced to imprisonment, the publisher was fined £500.

Speech & expression

Obscenity

Under the *Obscene Publications Act 1959*, it is an offence to publish material that is likely to "deprave and corrupt" someone who is likely to read, see or hear the material. However, this is a difficult subject to define, and what is considered obscene by the authorities can vary from one time to another.

Obscenity is normally associated with material of a sexual or pornographic nature – but may also include content and images of extreme violence.

Pornography involving children (ie young people under the age of 16) is dealt with very strictly in law. It is an offence to take, distribute, or possess an indecent photograph of a child.

New law

In 2005, the government announced plans to make it an offence to possess violent or abusive pornography, punishable by up to three years in prison. This means that it would become an offence for someone deliberately to view such material on a computer.

A government spokesman stated, "We do feel it necessary to provide some form of protection for the public, particularly for young children increasingly accessing the Internet. It is very important that we protect them from these kinds of extreme pornographic images." Those opposed to these measures argue that people ought to be allowed to make up their own minds about what they view.

Actions against the state

Restrictions on freedom of speech also apply to those who try to create public disorder or undermine the authority of the state. Action of this kind is an offence.

One of the oldest crimes of this type is treason – attempting to overthrow or betray one's country. Until 1998, anyone found guilty of treason in Britain could face the death penalty.

Other offences include trying to persuade someone in the police or armed forces not to do their duty. In 1973, Pat Arrowsmith and other peace campaigners distributed leaflets to soldiers, trying to persuade them not to serve in Northern Ireland, and giving them advice on how to desert. For this she was tried and found guilty under the *Incitement to Disaffection Act 1934*, and sentenced to prison for 18 months.

Terrorism

Recently the government has introduced a number of new anti-terrorism measures. For example, under the *Terrorism Act 2000*, it is an offence to incite or encourage someone to commit a terrorist act or to provide instructions or training in the use of firearms, explosives, or chemical, biological or nuclear weapons.

William Joyce

The last person to be executed for treason in Britain was William Joyce (known as Lord Haw-Haw). Born in 1906, he was a leading figure in the Fascist movement in Britain, very anti-Jewish, and a strong supporter of Hitler.

In 1939, shortly before the outbreak of war, William Joyce left the UK for Berlin where he started to work on the radio. For the next six years he regularly broadcast programmes to Britain on behalf of the Nazi government, designed to lower people's morale and make them believe that defeat by Germany was inevitable.

The British government made no attempt to jam or ban these broadcasts, and a lot of people listened to them. However few took him seriously and William Joyce became a figure of fun. He was arrested in northern Germany by British troops in 1945, brought to London and charged with treason. He was found guilty and executed the following year.

Speech & expression

 ## Censorship

Broadcasting

In Britain there is no direct state control over television and radio broadcasts. However, broadcasters are required, under the *Communications Act 2003*, to follow certain standards. These are laid down by the independent communications regulator called Ofcom – the Office for Communications.

These standards require that news is reported accurately and impartially, and that viewers and listeners are protected from harmful and offensive material. They also state that programmes should not glamorise anti-social behaviour, and that children are protected from unsuitable material.

Ofcom has a number of powers at its disposal if a programme fails to meet these standards. It can order that the programme is not shown again; it may shorten or take away the broadcaster's licence; or it may impose a fine of up to £250,000.

Wrong time

The BBC were heavily criticised by Ofcom for their daytime screening of a series of four programmes covering prostitution, pornography and drug-taking. Although warnings were given before each programme, Ofcom decided they did not adequately prepare viewers for the strength of the content at that time of day.

Government interference

There have been many occasions in the past when the government has intervened to try to prevent programmes being broadcast.

One of the earliest was in 1932, when the BBC planned to transmit a radio programme given by a former German U-boat captain about his experiences in the First World War. Lord Reith, the chairman of the BBC, was summoned by a government minister and told that the programme had to be withdrawn. If it was not, the minister explained, the planned royal

No talking

In 1988, under the *Broadcasting Act 1981*, the Home Secretary, Douglas Hurd, announced that radio and television stations in Britain were forbidden from broadcasting words spoken by people representing any one of eleven organisations in Northern Ireland believed to support terrorism. As a result, all statements made on television and radio by leaders of all the banned groups had to be spoken by actors.

The measures were debated and approved by both Houses of Parliament, but were challenged in court, going all the way up to the European Commission of Human Rights. Here it was decided that although the action limited freedom of expression, it was not unreasonable in the circumstances. The restrictions stayed in place until 1994 when the IRA agreed a ceasefire.

opening of the new Broadcasting House would be cancelled. Reluctantly, Lord Reith agreed.

In 1956, when Britain, France and Israel invaded Egypt over the Suez Canal, the Prime Minister, Anthony Eden, called on the BBC to support the war, and threatened a cut in their grant.

More recently, in the 1980s, both the BBC and ITV faced strong pressure from senior government ministers not to show programmes that put IRA leaders in a good light or were critical of British government policy in Northern Ireland.

National emergency

During times of national emergency, under the *Communications Act 2003*, the government may order a television or radio station to restrict or suspend broadcasts.

Newspapers

The government has no direct involvement in the newspaper business. Newspapers are privately owned by individuals or large companies and decisions about the content of articles are usually taken by the editor. Sometimes the owner or proprietor influences what is (and is not) published.

Newspapers do not have the same legal limits placed upon them as radio and television. They do not have to be fair and impartial and are free to support one political party in favour of another, as many do.

In the past

The printing press was first developed in Europe in the mid-1400s. For many years after this, newspapers and books printed in Britain were subject to heavy censorship – at first by the Church, and then the state. No book could be published without first being checked and approved. Although at times the law was ignored, the punishments for publishing without approval could be severe.

This particular form of censorship came to an end in 1695 when Parliament rejected King William III's wishes and refused to renew the *Printing Act*.

Speech & expression

Reporting restrictions

Journalists do not have the freedom to report all aspects of the news.

Official secrets

CARELESS TALK COSTS LIVES

It is an offence, under the *Official Secrets Acts*, to publish information that might be directly or indirectly useful to an enemy. This rule applies even if the journalist has been given the information by someone who works for the government or the Crown.

The law also forbids any former member of the security service from ever saying anything about their work.

Crimes and trials

In order to make sure that cases are dealt with in a just and fair manner, courts are – in general – open to the public. But, as most people cannot attend a trial or hearing in person, the media have the right to inform the public of what has taken place.

There are, however, certain exceptions to this – and therefore limits to freedom of speech. For example, if a young person under the age of 18 appears as a victim, witness or defendant in an adult court, the judge may order reporters not to give out any details that may lead to that person's identification. In youth courts, there is an automatic ban on publishing the name, address, or school of any child or young person appearing either as a witness or defendant.

In a similar way, it is an offence to publish or broadcast the name, address, or a picture of a woman or man who is a victim of rape.

No excuse

In 2002, David Shayler, a former MI5 officer, was jailed for six months after being found guilty of three charges of breaking the *Official Secrets Act*. He left the Secret Service in 1997, but before doing so, made copies of secret files that later became the basis for a number of articles about MI5 and MI6 published in a national newspaper.

In these articles Mr Shayler claimed that MI5 had carried out surveillance operations against politicians, who went on to become senior members of government, and others including John Lennon and members of the Sex Pistols. He also alleged that MI6 had been involved in a plot to assassinate the Libyan leader, Colonel Gaddafi. At his trial, Mr Shayler argued that it was in the public interest for people to know about important matters of this kind.

Mr Shayler was found guilty, but appealed to the House of Lords. However the judges rejected his appeal, stating that it was no defence for someone charged with breaking the *Official Secrets Act* to claim that they were acting in the public interest.

Film and theatre

Film

Film censorship in Britain is in the hands of local borough and county councils who decide whether a film can be shown in their area. Councils almost always follow the classification given by the British Board of Film Classification (BBFC).

The BBFC is an independent organisation that goes back to 1912, and was set up by the film industry as a way of trying to make sure that the government didn't get involved in film censorship. Today it classifies films, videos, DVDs and digital games (for example, U, PG, 15, 18, etc).

There are three main considerations in classifying a film. Is the material likely to:
- **break the law**
- **harm a particular age group**
- **be unacceptable to general public opinion?**

Today, relatively few films are cut – and where they are it is usually only to enable it to be given a lower age classification.

Theatre

Until 1968, the Lord Chamberlain (one of the chief officers of the Royal Household) was responsible for theatre censorship. This meant that he could require the wording of a play to be changed, sections removed and ban the staging of the play itself. His decision could not be challenged – not even by the House of Commons. This was because the Lord Chamberlain was a servant of the Royal Household and answerable only to the queen or king.

The power to censor plays was given to the Lord Chamberlain under the *Licensing Act 1737*. The Act was introduced by the Prime Minister, Robert Walpole, over his concern that political satire in the theatre was undermining him and the authority of his government.

Today there is no censor or classification system for stage plays. Instead, the only requirement is that they keep within law – and in particular that that are not obscene, give rise to racial hatred or cause a breach of the peace.

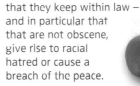

Privacy & information

AN INFORMATION SOCIETY

Privacy means being entitled to keep information about ourselves private from everyone other than those we choose to share it with. It is often argued that our privacy has come under pressure in recent years – with developments in technology and the tendency of many organisations to keep more detailed records than they did in the past. Privacy may also be threatened as the police and security forces try to deal with terrorism and the problems of international and organised crime.

However, although government departments and other public bodies hold a great deal of information, new laws now give people more rights to find out what that information is.

Is there a right to privacy?

There are a number of situations in which people may feel a loss of privacy. These include being photographed unknowingly or unwillingly, or having others know details of their finances, medical history, correspondence, telephone calls or personal relationships.

Loss of privacy may be due to actions by the state, commercial organisations or private individuals.

A patchwork of laws

There is no single law that protects people's privacy in Britain today, but there are a number of laws dealing with many of the circumstances in which a loss of privacy might arise. Some of these protections go back many years. The laws of trespass are amongst the oldest – restricting the right of people to enter private property without the proper authority to do so.

NPG D2310 John Entick
by W.P. Benoist, after Burgess
Date: published 1763 Medium: line engraving
© National Portrait Gallery, London

The way we were

On 11th November 1762, four messengers of the King broke into the house of John Entick in Stepney, east London, and for the next four hours searched his house, examining all his private papers. When the messengers left they took with them more than a hundred papers and charts.

John Entick was a teacher and had written a number of newspaper articles criticising the government. Ministers wanted this to stop, and the Home Secretary of the time, the Second Earl of Halifax, issued a warrant for Entick's house to be searched.

John Entick sued the messengers for trespass to his house. They claimed that their warrant gave them full authority to carry out the search. In court, the judge disagreed. He said that only Parliament could issue a warrant of this type – not ministers – and that the search had therefore been unlawful. The messengers had no authority to be on John Entick's property. The judge stated, "If it is law, it will be found in our books. If it is not to be found there, it is not law. No man can set his foot upon my ground without my license [permission]. If he admits the fact, he is bound to shew by way of justification, that some positive law has empowered or excused him." The judge could find no excuse for the messengers' behaviour, and John Entick was awarded damages.

Privacy & information

The protection of rights

Article 8 of the European Convention on Human Rights protects a person's private and family life, their home and correspondence from interference by the state. This has been incorporated into UK law by the *Human Rights Act 1998*.

This freedom from interference by the state is not absolute, however. The state may interfere with a person's privacy to protect the public interest (for example, for reasons of national security or public safety) and when there is the authority in law to do so. But it cannot act in an arbitrary manner. Actions of public authorities, like the police and security forces, must remain within the law.

The European Convention on Human Rights, Article 8

"Everyone has the right to respect for his private and family life, his home and correspondence.

"There shall be no interference by a public authority with the exercise of this right except such as is in accordance with the law and is necessary in a democratic society in the interests of national security, public safety or the economic well-being of the country, for the prevention of disorder or crime, for the protection of health or morals, or for the protection of rights and freedoms of others."

◖ Privacy and the police

Entry and search

Today, generally speaking, the powers of the police to enter and search a person's property are set out in the *Police and Criminal Evidence Act 1984* (sometimes known as PACE).

Without a warrant

The police can enter a property without a search warrant for a number of reasons. These include to:

- **make an arrest in connection with a serious offence, such as robbery or serious assault,**
- **look for evidence in connection with someone who has already been arrested,**
- **catch an escaped prisoner, save life, or to prevent serious damage or disturbance.**

Privacy & information

Warrant required

If the police wish to search a property in most other circumstances, they need to obtain a search warrant from a magistrate or judge. On certain occasions, however, for example in connection with terrorism or the *Official Secrets Act*, permission may instead be given by a police officer of the rank of superintendent or above, if immediate action is required.

Warrants may not be given for certain kinds of searches. For example, the police do not generally have the right to see confidential personal health records or details of conversations between a lawyer and their client.

A search must only be for the purpose for which the warrant was issued. It does not allow the police to carry out a general search. Before entering the property and making the search, the police should, if it is possible, explain their reasons to the occupant, and should use no more force than is reasonable in the circumstances.

Damage

If the police cause damage in entering or searching a building, they are normally required to explain to the owner or occupier how to apply for compensation.

The payment of damages, for repairs etc, depends on the circumstances of each case. Compensation is unlikely to be paid if the police can show that they searched the premises in a lawful and reasonable way. Damages are normally obtainable only if the police have made a mistake and searched the wrong premises, or actually had no right in law to carry out the search.

Too far

In 1997, police officers investigating a possible case of fraud, obtained warrants to search the offices and stores of a number of people under suspicion. The scope of these warrants was very wide – and allowed the police to collect almost any evidence they liked. As a result, documents and papers of all kinds were taken, as were items of clothing and family photographs. Objections to this were raised by those whose offices had been searched, and they asked a court to order the return of those items that had been unfairly taken.

The judges decided that the search warrants that had been issued gave the police far too much freedom in what they could search for and take. They believed that the true purpose of the search was not to support the investigation, but to help the police put together a case against the suspects. The judges therefore decided that the search was unlawful.

Surveillance by the State

Placing a person under surveillance – that is, watching or listening to what they are doing – is not in itself against the law. The legal position depends on the circumstances in which the surveillance takes place.

Developments in technology, particularly over the last 30 years, have provided the police and other state organisations with increasingly effective ways of carrying out surveillance. Bugging devices, secret cameras, access to telephone conversations and e-mail messages, may all provide evidence in the investigation of crime.

However, until 1985 there were no laws that specifically protected people's privacy from surveillance. There were rules and procedures that the police were expected to follow, but they did not have the force of law. Today this has changed, and surveillance by the police and other government bodies is largely controlled by two laws – the *Police Act 1997* and the *Regulation of Investigatory Powers Act 2000*.

No protection

In 1979, antique dealer, James Malone, was charged with handling stolen goods. During the trial, it became clear that the police had gathered evidence for the case by tapping his telephone and listening to his conversations. Mr Malone was found not guilty and acquitted of the charge, but after the trial brought his own case against the police – claiming that tapping his calls had been illegal and an interference with his privacy.

The judge said that, as the law stood, the police had done nothing illegal. Mr Malone then took his case to the European Court of Human Rights. Here the judges decided that UK law did not adequately control the ways in which telephone tapping was carried out and therefore broke Article 8 of the European Convention on Human Rights.

As a result of this judgement, the British government was required to introduce new laws controlling the ways in which telephone tapping could take place.

Privacy & information

Observation and listening devices

Under the *Police Act 1997*, the police have powers to enter premises and install secret spying or surveillance equipment. The authorisation to do this can only be given by someone of the rank of chief constable, and should be in writing – unless the case is very urgent.

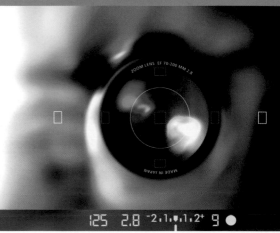

If the camera or listening device is to be installed in a dwelling, hotel bedroom, or office, permission from a Surveillance Commissioner is also required – unless the matter is so urgent that this cannot be obtained until after the device is installed. The Surveillance Commissioner is a serving or retired High Court judge.

Other state organisations, as well as the police, have the power to carry out surveillance activities. Most need to obtain permission in advance. These include the Dept of Health, Work and Pensions, the Dept of Environment, Food and Rural Affairs, HM Revenue & Customs, the Foods Standard Agency, and the security services.

In 2003/4 approximately 30,000 surveillance authorisations were issued. About 3,000 of these involved secret surveillance inside a person's home or car.

The circumstances in which surveillance can take place are set out in law. Intrusive surveillance, such as hiding a listening device or camera in someone's home, may be carried out only for reasons of national security, the protection of the economic well-being of the UK, or the prevention or detection of serious crime.

Tip off

Several local councils in England and Wales use hidden cameras to try to catch fly-tippers – people who dump old items like beds and tyres in the countryside. As soon as they get a warning that someone is leaving rubbish in a particular area, the council installs a hidden camera on the site, hoping to catch the culprit and to have evidence with which to take that person to court.

Complaints

Anyone who is concerned that they have been placed under surveillance can make a complaint to the Investigatory Powers Tribunal. The Tribunal can order that the surveillance must stop, that the information obtained is destroyed, and may also award compensation to the victim, see also **www.ipt-uk.com**.

If the police break the law in the way in which they obtain surveillance information a court may decide that the case against the accused cannot continue.

Not allowed

In December 2000, the remains of a 23-year-old man were found on remote farmland near Darlington in Co Durham. They were identified as the body of a man who had disappeared six months earlier, and post-mortem tests showed that he had died from gunshot wounds. He was believed to have been the victim of a gangland execution, and five men were charged with his murder.

A week before the five men were arrested, the police applied for permission to install hidden listening devices at the police station where the suspects would be held. There is nothing unusual in this, but one of the areas where the bugs were located was the exercise yard, where discussion between the accused and their solicitors often took place. It is against the law for the police to eavesdrop on a private conversation between solicitors and their clients. When the judge hearing the case realised that this had taken place he decided that the trial could not go ahead. The five men accused of murder were freed.

Privacy & information

CCTV cameras

Most British towns and cities have close circuit cameras in public areas. Reports indicate that there are as many as four million CCTV cameras in use in public spaces in Britain – more than anywhere else in the world, relative to its population. Cameras are located in many places where there is public access, including shopping centres, residential streets, hospitals, airports, and alongside motorways. The main reason for their installation is the prevention and detection of crime.

Unlike most other European countries, there is no law in Britain regulating or controlling the installation of CCTV cameras. Public bodies – such as the police and local councils – may install as many cameras as they wish. Unlike other fixtures, like large shop signs, the installation of CCTV cameras does not require planning permission.

There are regulations, however, affecting the ways in which the cameras are operated and how the film may be used. For example, street cameras installed by a local authority must be programmed not to invade people's privacy by looking into their houses, and the film may only be used in the prevention and detection of crime.

Using the images

Late one night, in August 1995, a man tried to commit suicide by slashing his wrists in the high street of a town in Essex. Council CCTV cameras installed nearby recorded the moment shortly after this, showing him in a very distressed state, still holding the knife and bleeding profusely. The emergency services were immediately called; the man was treated, and then allowed home.

A few months later, images of this were shown on local television and released to the papers as part of a publicity campaign promoting the benefits of CCTV in the fight against crime. The face of the man had not been properly blanked out and was recognised by neighbours and colleagues.

The man involved took his case to court, claiming that the council were breaking the law by using the film in this way. The court disagreed, saying that the council was legally entitled to act as it did.

The case was then taken to the European Court of Human Rights, where the judges reached a different conclusion, deciding that the man's right to privacy, as set out in Article 8 of the European Convention, had been broken. The council, the Court stated, could have asked the man's permission to use the film or used other film for the same purpose. The man was awarded £8,000 in damages.

Intercepting communications

If the police, customs officers, or the secret security service want to intercept a letter, telephone call, fax or e-mail, they normally need a warrant to do so. (A warrant is a legal document, in this case, usually signed by the Home Secretary.)

There are some situations, however, when a warrant is not required. These include tapping into telephone conversations in a prison, young offenders' institution, or remand centre, secure psychiatric hospitals, hospitals in Scotland and into communications outside the UK.

Not in court

Information gained from telephone taps may be useful in the investigation of crime and the prevention of terrorism. In the UK, the information may be used for intelligence purposes – but not as evidence in court. Britain is quite unusual in this respect.

Keeping a check

The Prime Minister is required by law to appoint a senior judge to check that the power to intercept communications is not abused. The judge is known as the Interception of Communications Commissioner. Currently, he or she visits twice yearly those organisations with the power to tap telephones to see how they carry out their work and to check some of the warrants that have been issued.

The Commissioner prepares a report on this work each year for the Prime Minister, which is presented to Parliament – with certain parts removed, for reasons of national security.

Is my phone being tapped?

It is not possible for a person to find out if their phone is being tapped. Neither the police nor intelligence services have a duty to reveal whether a warrant has been issued authorising a phone tap.

Telephone, e-mail and Internet records

Telephone numbers people have called, where the calls have been made, the people to whom they have sent e-mails, and Internet sites they have visited all provide details of the way people live their lives.

Information of this kind can now be made available to a wide number of public organisations. As well as the police and security services, the list now includes HM Revenue & Customs, the fire and ambulance services, the Health Service, local councils and the immigration service. Access requires the approval of a senior member of the organisation. In the case of the police, it is someone of the rank of inspector or above.

Unlike intercepted communications, details of a person's telephone records may be used as evidence in court.

Companies providing telephone, e-mail and Internet services are now required to keep customers' records available for inspection for a period of at least a year.

Privacy & information

Personal records and the State

Personal records have been collected by the State for hundreds of years. Records of births, marriages and deaths – dating back as far as the 1600s – may be found in the registers of some of the oldest churches in England and Wales.

Many other records are now held by the state. Anyone who drives a car, pays taxes, has a passport, is registered to vote, or buys a house has their details held by one or more government organisations. Even babies have an NHS number.

Police files

The Police National Computer is the central database for police forces throughout England, Wales and Northern Ireland.

It holds extensive details on:
- **prosecutions, convictions, and cautions**
- **people wanted or missing**
- **vehicle owners**
- **disqualified drivers**
- **stolen vehicles and property**
- **fingerprints.**

It has the capacity to identify similarities in incidents, to carry out searches on the basis of personal characteristics, such as accents, nicknames, shoe size, and types of offence, and to identify, for example, all the vehicles registered to people living in a particular street.

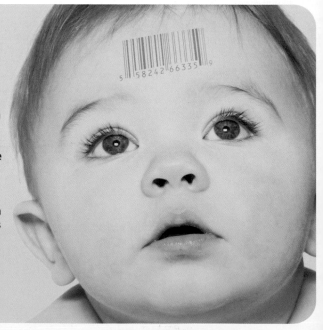

Keeping count

The UK's first census (an official count of the population) took place in 1801, but it wasn't until 1837 in England and Wales (1855 in Scotland) that births, marriages and deaths were officially registered. It became compulsory to register the birth of a child in 1875.

The information given on birth certificates includes the child's name, sex and date of birth; their mother's and father's names, dates and places of birth, their occupation; details of the mother's marriage, and her usual address.

Matching numbers

Cameras located on many major roads scan the registration numbers of the thousands of vehicles that pass by each day. These are automatically checked against police records to identify those of particular interest to the police.

The same technology is now being used on garage forecourts, partly as a means of catching those who drive off without paying for their fuel, but also to provide the police with a 24-hour intelligence feed.

How long are records held?

A record of a person's convictions normally remains on the Police National Computer for at least ten years.

If the person has three or more convictions for imprisonable offences, the record will be kept for at least 20 years and, in some circumstances, for life. This includes anyone who has been given prison sentences totalling six months or more, been convicted of a sexual, violent, or serious drug offence, or convicted of an offence involving a child or vulnerable adult.

The Home Office states that records of cautions, reprimands and final warnings should generally be kept until the offender is 18, or for five years – whichever is longer.

Can I check my record?

Anyone who wishes to check the contents of their police record may obtain an application form either from a police station or via the local police force website. Proof of identity is required, along with a £10 search fee. Details of this are available from **www.police.uk**.

DNA database

DNA – a record of each person's unique inherited characteristics – is a valuable tool in detecting or eliminating people suspected of committing a crime.

During an investigation the police may take samples of DNA from suspects and witnesses. These records are stored on a large database. There is no limit on the time which they may be kept. They are not destroyed at the end of the investigation, even if the suspect has been eliminated from police enquiries.

On the record

A group of young people got on a bus in Glasgow and refused to pay their fare. An argument followed and they were ordered off by the driver, but not before one of the youths, aged 17, had spat in his face and shouted racist remarks.

A sample of the young man's saliva was checked against police DNA records. On the basis of this, and three witness statements, he was found guilty of assault and racially aggravated breach of the peace, and fined £300.

Privacy & information

Access to information

The development of computer technology over the past 30 years has enabled public bodies, companies and other organisations to store large amounts of information about their clients, customers and staff.

Whilst this information may be an important tool for administration or business, there is a possibility that it may be inaccurate or misused in some way. The *Data Protection Act 1998* is designed to prevent this by setting out certain rules that people holding personal information stored on a computer (or paper filing system) must follow.

Until recently in Britain, there has never been a general right of access to information held by public bodies, such as government departments or local councils. This changed with the creation of the *Freedom of Information Act 2000*, which allows anyone to ask more than 100,000 public bodies for information that they hold.

Data protection

Many organisations hold information about people – name, address, earnings, medical details, education records etc. Difficulties arise if the information is inaccurate or used in some way against the person's wishes.

Under the *Data Protection Act* anyone storing personal information (other than about their family or household) must register with the Information Commissioner's Office, indicating the type of information that is held, and the uses to which it is put. Individuals and organisations holding personal data must also follow a code of practice, requiring them to make sure the information held is accurate, secure, properly used, not excessive and not kept for longer than necessary.

My rights
People have the right to find out what information is held about them by a wide range of organisations. These include public bodies such as social services, the local housing authority, schools, and health services; also employers, banks and credit agencies.

The information may be held in either computer or paper records. It also, with some exceptions, includes personal information held in e-mails.

Some personal data does not have to be given. For example, the police and tax authorities do not have to disclose information that may damage national security or may affect the way in which crime is detected or taxes collected. In some cases, a person's rights to see files held on them by their doctor or social worker may also be limited.

Obtaining information
If you wish to check any personal information that is held about you by an organisation or individual, you may write to them and ask for a copy. They have 40 days in which to reply. If the information is incorrect, irrelevant, or out of date, you may ask to have it changed or removed. If you are unable to sort out the problem yourself, you can ask for help from the Information Commissioner's Office. Usually the office tries to sort out the problem informally, but it can take action against an individual or organisation to make sure that the law is properly followed. See also **www.ico.gov.uk**.

Freedom of information

The *Freedom of Information Act 2000* gives you the right to ask for official information held by public authorities. If you feel that a public authority has wrongly withheld information, you can complain to the Information Commissioner's Office, see page 50.

The Act came into force in 2005, and one of the main reasons for its existence is to make government more open and transparent. It applies to all public authorities in England, Wales and Northern Ireland. There is separate legislation for Scotland. Public authorities include government departments, local councils, the police, the NHS, schools, universities – and all kinds of other government bodies, such as the British Museum, the Meat and Livestock Commission and the Sports Council for Wales.

Requests

Applications should be made in writing (by letter or e-mail), and the organisation is normally required to respond within 20 working days. There may be a charge for the information, and if the request is refused an appeal can be made to the Information Commissioner's Office.

Information withheld

Certain information is absolutely exempted and may not be released. This is likely to be for reasons of national security or because it is protected by other laws such as the *Data Protection Act*. There are also specific types of information that can be withheld, such as information for future publications, trade secrets and communications with the Queen and other members of the royal family.

One of the tests that is applied in deciding whether to release information is whether it is more in the public interest for it to be released or withheld.

Revealed under the Act

Requests for information under the *Freedom of Information Act* have covered all kinds of topics. It has been revealed under the Act that one of the inspectors investigating the collapse of MG Rover charged nearly £12,000 a day for three months' work; that the Great Western Hospital in Swindon took £1.2m in parking fees over three years; and that the cancer-causing chemical cadmium was released over Norwich by government scientists in the 1960s to test how it would disperse in the air.

Citizenship, immigration & asylum

RIGHTS AND DUTIES

The word "citizenship" today generally refers to membership of the country to which a person belongs – and is something that can have a very significant effect on their life.

British citizenship gives people certain legal rights – such as the right to enter and remain in Britain, to hold a passport, to vote, and to work. It entitles them to protection from the state and gives access to the full range of social benefits.

Citizenship also brings certain duties and obligations. These include loyalty, which means not plotting against the state, and certain civic responsibilities, such as voting and jury service. In some countries, although not the UK, civic duties include helping to defend the country through military and other service.

Every state can, through its laws and constitution, decide who may and may not enter the country, and may remove anyone who stays unlawfully – as long as it keeps to any international agreements that it has already made.

Military service

Many countries have compulsory military service, but it is usually for men only. China is one of the few countries where both men and women are called up for military service. The service period is normally from 9–18 months.

In some countries, such as Germany, conscientious objectors (those objecting to military service) are offered alternative civilian service.

Compulsory service existed in Britain during the First and Second World Wars, and national service, as it was known after the War, continued until 1960.

Citizenship

Britain's laws on nationality and citizenship tend to be more complicated than those of many other countries, and have been shaped by events in the past.

The King's subjects

As far back as the fourteenth century, anyone born within land controlled by the King of England automatically became a subject under his control. Additionally, anyone born overseas whose father was an English subject also became a subject themselves.

The growth of an empire

During the seventeenth, eighteenth and nineteenth centuries, Britain acquired many territories overseas, known as colonies. This resulted in the creation of a large Empire, covering many parts of Africa, the Indian sub-continent, Australia, New Zealand and parts of the Far East, North, Central and South America. Anyone who lived in these countries was automatically a British subject. This was later confirmed in an Act of Parliament, the *British Nationality and Status of Aliens Act 1914* – and this arrangement continued until 1948.

From Empire to Commonwealth

During the twentieth century, many British colonies obtained independence, but almost all chose to keep some kind of link with Britain. This gave rise to an association of states, known as the Commonwealth, see page 111.

As these states became independent, each created its own national citizenship. In 1948, however, it was also agreed that people living in Britain and the Commonwealth would also be given the status of *Citizen of the United Kingdom and Colonies*. This was designed to make sure that no one was without some form of citizenship and allowed Commonwealth citizens to enter and live in the UK.

During the 1960s, concerns developed in the UK over the number of people from Commonwealth countries who were coming to settle in Britain. Tighter controls were introduced, with the aim of reducing the numbers of those entitled to live in the UK. Further restrictions were put in place in 1981, resulting in Commonwealth citizens no longer having the status of British subjects.

The *British Nationality Act 1981* created three categories of British citizenship: British citizenship, citizenship of British dependent territories, and British overseas citizenship. Of these, only British citizenship provides the right to live in the UK.

Citizenship, immigration & asylum

British citizenship today

Today, generally speaking, a person may become a British citizen in one of five ways.

Born in the UK Since 1983, a person automatically becomes a British citizen if they are:
- **born in the UK, and**
- **their parents are married, and**
- **at least one of their parents is a British citizen, or settled in the UK.**

A person born in the UK, whose parents are not married, becomes a UK citizen if their mother is a British citizen or is settled in the UK.

Adoption A child, who is adopted by a British citizen, becomes a British citizen on the day of the adoption order.

Descent If a child with a British parent is born outside the UK, then that child becomes a British citizen – as long as the parent did not acquire their citizenship by descent. If they did, then the child will have British citizenship only if that parent was working overseas for the UK government or European Community.

Registration A child born in the UK, but not registered for British citizenship, may, at the age of ten, qualify for British citizenship, as long as they have not spent more than 90 days a year outside the UK.

A child may also become a British citizen if their parent gains British citizenship.

Naturalisation This is the process by which a person who is of another nationality applies to become a British citizen.

Becoming British

In order to become a British citizen through naturalisation, there are certain requirements that a person must follow.

1. **Arrive in Britain.**
2. **Live in Britain for five years (three years if married to a British national).**
3. **Have some understanding of the English (or Welsh or Gaelic) language and British culture, and pass a language and knowledge test.**
4. **Apply to become a British citizen, paying a fee of between £120 and £150. Wait for a decision.**
5. **Receive British citizenship at a public ceremony.**

New citizen

Larissa came to Britain from Ukraine in 1999, to study for a degree. She met and married a British man on her course, and today lives and works in London. She speaks good English and, in 2005, took and passed the exam testing her knowledge of UK life. Shortly afterwards, at a ceremony at her local town hall, Larissa was made a British citizen.

Citizenship ceremonies

Since 2004, like many other countries, Britain has required all new UK citizens, over the age of 18, to attend a citizenship ceremony held in their local town or city.

During the ceremony, each new citizen either swears an oath of allegiance or makes an affirmation of allegiance to the Queen. They also make a pledge of commitment to the United Kingdom.

Unnecessary

A registrar in Rochdale, Lancashire, said that he would refuse to carry out citizenship ceremonies in which migrants to the UK are formally given British citizenship. "People should not be forced to take part in these ceremonies against their will," he said. "How many people in this country would take an oath of allegiance to the Queen? I know I wouldn't. People who come and live in the UK may well disagree with the royal family. They should not be forced to take part in a ceremony they disagree with."

Citizenship, immigration & asylum

Ending British citizenship

A person who decides that they no longer wish to be a British citizen can do so only if they have obtained citizenship or nationality of another state. Anyone who has not done this within six months of giving up their British citizenship officially remains a British citizen. These measures are designed to prevent people from being stateless and having nowhere they can legally live.

Losing British citizenship

Under the *Nationality and Asylum Act 2002*, the Home Secretary has the power to take away a person's British citizenship. This applies to all British citizens, including those born in the UK.

There are two general reasons why this may be done. The first is they have behaved in a way that seriously damages the interests of the UK or its overseas territories. The second is because of fraud or deceit in obtaining citizenship.

A person who is about to lose their citizenship has the right of appeal – although this may not apply if the Home Secretary decides that the reasons for citizenship being withdrawn should not be disclosed.

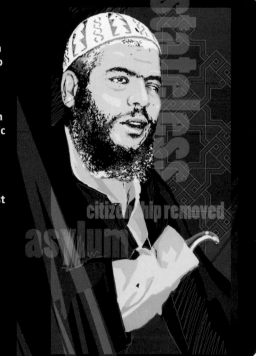

Stripped of citizenship?

Abu Hamza al-Masri was the first person to be deprived of their British citizenship under the *Nationality and Asylum Act 2002*. The then Home Secretary, David Blunkett, issued papers in 2003 withdrawing Abu Hamza's citizenship on the grounds that the Egyptian-born cleric had encouraged, advised and trained people to take up terrorist activities against Britain.

Lawyers for Abu Hamza appealed against this decision on the grounds that their client would become stateless if he lost his British citizenship. In 2006, Abu Hamza was found guilty of inciting his followers to murder and racial hatred, and sentenced to seven years in prison. At the time of his trial, no decision had been reached on Abu Hamza's citizenship.

Passports and travel

Eight hundred years ago, the *Magna Carta* (see page 10) gave citizens freedom to enter, leave, travel and stay in England, although in times of emergency, this could be suspended by order of the king.

Today, the right to leave and enter Britain still exists. However, in practice, it is very difficult to do so without a passport – and there is no automatic legal right for a UK citizen to obtain a passport. The issue of withdrawal of passports is controlled by the Crown, (acting through the Identity and Passport Service) and not through laws passed by Parliament.

It is rare for passports to be taken away from people, but when this takes place it is done on the decision of the Home Secretary, using the Royal Prerogative, see page 74.

Citizenship of the European Union

Britain's membership of the European Union means that British citizens are also citizens of the European Union. As a result, UK citizens have the right to travel, work and live within any of the 25 states of the European Union. EU citizens living in the UK also have rights to vote in local and European elections, see page 106.

Refused

Four British men, who were released and returned to Britain after being held in Guantanamo Bay, were refused passports by the Home Secretary. A letter to each of the men from the Home Office stated that passports were not being issued because of the fear that they would take part in activities against the UK from abroad.

Citizenship, immigration & asylum

Immigration

Until just over 100 years ago, Britain had open borders, with few restrictions on those who could come into the country. This did not mean, however, that outsiders (or aliens, as they were known) have always been welcome.

Sometimes the law has reflected strong prejudices held against particular groups of people. In 1290, Edward I ordered the expulsion of all Jewish people from Britain – some of whom were aliens, but many were British subjects. In 1530, a law was passed banning the entry of Gypsies. In 1547, this was extended to give all Gypsies over the age of 14 born in England just one month to leave the country.

Limits on entry have also been placed during times of war and political instability. When Ireland helped Spain in the war against England, Queen Elizabeth I issued a proclamation that "no manner of person born in the realm of Ireland ... shall remain in the realm."
Following the French Revolution, laws controlled the entry of travellers from France between 1793 and 1826, fearing that they might bring their revolutionary fervour to England.

What rights do people have to come to Britain?

Much of the law controlling immigration to Britain is controlled by the *Immigration Act 1971*. In simple terms, it divides people into two categories: those that have an automatic right to live and work in the UK, and those who require permission to do so.

Generally, those with an automatic right to enter and live in the UK are:
- **British citizens**
- **some Commonwealth citizens**
- **citizens of EU states, see page 105**
- **citizens of Iceland, Liechtenstein, Norway and Switzerland**
- **Irish citizens.**

Those people from countries where there is not an automatic right to enter and stay in Britain need to apply for permission to stay for a limited or indefinite period, and may face certain restrictions. These may, for example, limit their period of stay or right to work, or require them to register with the police.

Appeals
People who are refused entry to Britain, or are required to leave, can under some (but not all) circumstances appeal against the decision.

Their case will be heard by one or more immigration judges at an Asylum and Immigration Tribunal. For more details see the Tribunal's website, **www.ait.gov.uk**.

Asylum

Asylum means a place of safety and protection. Under international law, someone who fears or faces persecution in their own country has the right to seek asylum (or refuge) elsewhere. A person who seeks asylum in Britain is asking for the right to be recognised as a refugee and to enter and stay in this country legally.

Protection under international and national law

The *United Nations Convention on Refugees* came into force in 1954. It is an international agreement, signed by Britain and most other countries in the world, promising to give protection to people who flee their country because of persecution. States signing this document also agree, under international law, not to return a refugee from the country they left if that person's freedom or life is likely to be threatened because of their race, religion, nationality, membership of a particular social group or political opinion.

In Britain, refugees are also protected by the *Human Rights Act 1998*, under which the state has a duty to protect people from torture, inhuman or degrading treatment.

No return

Gideon came to Britain from Zimbabwe in 2002. In 2005 he applied for asylum, claiming that as a member of the MDC opposition party in Zimbabwe his life would be in great danger if he returned home.

However, when British officials asked Gideon what the letters MDC stood for, and what were the names of his party's leaders, he was unable to answer. He was refused asylum.

When Gideon appealed against this decision, the chairman of the Immigration and Appeal Tribunal decided that even though Gideon had lied to the British authorities, he still had a "well-founded fear of persecution" if he returned to Zimbabwe. Gideon, and a number of other asylum seekers from Zimbabwe, were allowed to stay in Britain.

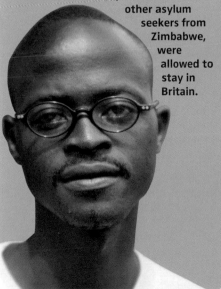

Citizenship, immigration & asylum

Applying for asylum

A person can apply for asylum in Britain either as they enter the country (at the airport, seaport or railway station) or, once they are inside the country, at a government immigration control office.

Every case depends on the circumstances of the person making the application. But, generally speaking, an asylum seeker needs to meet the requirements of the UN Convention on Refugees. This means that they must have:

- **a well-founded fear of being persecuted for reasons of race, religion, nationality, membership of a particular social group, or political opinion; and**
- **are unable or, because of that fear, unwilling to avail themselves of the protection of that country.** (From the *UN Convention on Refugees*.)

An asylum seeker may not be removed from the UK until a decision on their application has been reached.

Accommodation and detention

Most asylum seekers are allowed to live freely in the UK, as long as they give their address and regularly report to the authorities. There are powers however, to hold asylum seekers in detention centres (or in prisons) whilst their application is being considered.

Asylum seekers can be required to stay in a specific area, and must inform the Home Office if they change their address. Failure to do this or to report regularly to the authorities reduces the applicant's chances of success and may result in the removal of support.

Fear and persecution

When Kamaria was 23, her father was murdered and her husband imprisoned for their political activities. Kamaria believed that her own life was in danger and decided to flee the town in Somalia, where she had lived all her life. When she reached Britain she applied for asylum. It took three years for a decision to be reached, and she was eventually given refugee status. Kamaria now works at a school in Sheffield.

Refusal

If a person's claim for asylum is rejected, they will generally have a right to appeal, unless they have come from a country that the Home Office judges to be safe.

Similarly, an asylum seeker who has travelled through a safe country on the way to the UK may be sent back to that country to claim asylum there. It is only possible to appeal against this decision once the asylum seeker has left the UK.

More information on the process of claiming asylum is available from the Community Legal Service Direct, **www.clsdirect.org.uk** and clicking on *free legal information leaflets*.

Deportation

Deportation refers to the expulsion of someone from the United Kingdom. A British citizen cannot be deported and nor, in some circumstances, can Irish and Commonwealth citizens. Citizens from EU states may be deported from Britain.

A person may be deported from Britain for a number of reasons – for example, because:

- **their application for asylum has failed**
- **their work permit or visa has expired**
- **the Home Secretary believes that their deportation would be for the public good**
- **someone in their family is also being deported**
- **they have committed a serious crime, and deportation has been recommended by the court.**

Not in Britain

Farid and Feriba came to Britain with their two children, hidden in the back of a lorry. They had originally come from Afghanistan, where they faced great danger from violence and persecution, but had spent several weeks in Germany before finally reaching England. Although they said that they preferred life in Britain, their application for asylum in the UK was turned down by the Home Office and the family returned to Germany – the first safe country through which they had passed.

Equality

EQUALITY AND FREEDOM FROM DISCRIMINATION

Ideas about equality have changed greatly through history. Many societies in the past (and some still today) were based on principles of inequality, rather than equality. Society was often seen as a hierarchy or pyramid, with a small number of people at the top enjoying special rights and powers, given to them by birth.

It was during the seventeenth, eighteenth and nineteenth centuries that the idea of equality started to become established in Britain, but many groups remained unequal. Slavery was not outlawed until 1807, and women in Britain did not obtain equal rights to vote until 1928. Many of the laws we have today outlawing discrimination in work, housing and other situations have only been introduced in the last 30 years.

Equality, however, is not only about equal rights to vote or work. It is also an important requirement of a fair and just legal system. All people should be equal under the law, whatever their social position. This was set out as far back as 1215 in the *Magna Carta* (see page 10), with the words: "To no one will we sell, to no one deny or delay right or justice."

The principle of equality before the law is also established in Article 14 of the European Convention on Human Rights, incorporated into UK law by the *Human Rights Act 1998*. This states that the rights under the European Convention (see page 110) must be available to all, without discrimination – unless a restriction can be reasonably justified.

The European Convention on Human Rights, Article 14

"The enjoyment of the rights and freedoms … shall be secured without discrimination on any ground such as sex, race, colour, language, political or other opinion, national or social origin, association with a national minority, property, birth or other status."

Equality under the law

Everyone is equal

In 2001, footballers Lee Bowyer and Jonathan Woodgate were among four people charged with causing an affray and committing grievous bodily harm on Sarfraz Najeib, who was beaten unconscious in an attack outside a Leeds nightclub.

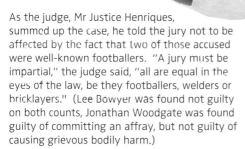

As the judge, Mr Justice Henriques, summed up the case, he told the jury not to be affected by the fact that two of those accused were well-known footballers. "A jury must be impartial," the judge said, "all are equal in the eyes of the law, be they footballers, welders or bricklayers." (Lee Bowyer was found not guilty on both counts, Jonathan Woodgate was found guilty of committing an affray, but not guilty of causing grievous bodily harm.)

An important principle of a fair and just society is that all people are equal in the eyes of the law. Everyone, regardless of their position in society, must obey the law, and those who are found to have broken the law should be treated in similar ways. This means that although the police have powers that other citizens do not, police officers who break the law risk facing charges in the same way as anyone else. Generally speaking, no one in Britain is above the law – although there are some exceptions, see page 64.

Any other passenger

Early one morning in January 2000, Cherie Booth QC, a lawyer and judge, and the wife of Prime Minister, Tony Blair, was running late for a business appointment. She boarded a train at Blackfriars station in London to travel to Luton, 30 miles away.

When she got off the train and reached the barriers at Luton, Ms Booth told the ticket collector that she didn't have a ticket. She explained that the ticket office at the station in London was closed and that she was unable to buy a ticket from a machine because she only had a small amount of cash in her purse and the ticket machine would not take credit cards.

Before she could leave the station, Ms Booth was required to pay £9.70, the cost of her ticket, plus an on-the-spot penalty of £10. A spokesman for the train company said later, "Ms Booth told the ticket collector at Luton that she didn't have a ticket and was dealt with as any other passenger would have been."

Equality

The Queen and the law

When a person is charged with a crime and the case comes to court – the case is listed as 'R v the surname' of the accused, eg *R v Smith*.

The R stands for *Regina* (the Latin for 'queen') or for *Rex* (the Latin for 'king'). This particular form of words reflects the fact that the charge against the accused is being taken in the name of the queen or king, on behalf of the state.

One consequence of administering justice in the name of the monarch is that the monarch cannot be prosecuted (the Queen couldn't prosecute herself), nor can he or she be required to give evidence in court.

This is known as Crown immunity and refers to those situations in which the queen or king, government departments, ministers and the armed forces are outside (or immune from) the law.

This position does not extend, however, to all members of the royal family. For example, in 2000, Princess Anne was fined £400 for speeding at 93mph and, two years later, appeared in court charged under the *Dangerous Dogs Act 1991*, after one of her dogs had bitten two children enjoying a day out in Windsor Park. Princess Anne pleaded guilty and was fined £500, and ordered to pay £500 compensation.

Government, ministers, and the civil service

Until the late 1940s, government departments and officials could neither be prosecuted nor sued for accidents or damage arising from their mistakes. This meant that someone injured through the error of a public body or official would find it very difficult to obtain compensation.

Today, public bodies are generally responsible for their mistakes in much the same way as private organisations and individuals. This means that all government bodies have to follow health and safety laws – but unlike private companies, they cannot be held *criminally* liable for their mistakes.

Diplomats

A diplomat is an official representative of their country overseas. A senior diplomat is usually known as an 'ambassador'.

Diplomats have traditionally had special rights and protections in international law. These include the right not to have their premises, correspondence and baggage inspected; immunity from criminal prosecution; and the right not to pay taxes and custom duties in the country in which they are working.

These rights are set out in the *1961 Vienna Convention on Diplomatic Relations* and are designed to ensure diplomats' safety and to protect them from mistreatment.

A diplomat who breaks the law of the country in which he or she is working cannot normally be taken to court. However, under certain circumstances immunity is waived by the home country, or the diplomat sent home and dealt with there. A victim may also bring an action against the diplomat in his or her own country.

No prosecution

In 2001, John Wynne was killed while working at the Royal Mint in Llantrisant in south Wales. He was crushed to death beneath a six and a half ton furnace, carrying metal to be made into coins. An investigation into the accident revealed that the furnace had fallen a distance of about four metres from a crane hook that was already known to be damaged. A health and safety inspector told the inquiry that, with proper care and planning, the accident would not have occurred.

There was strong evidence in this case that the Royal Mint had broken health and safety law. Normally this would result in the company facing a trial and the likelihood of a very heavy fine. However the Royal Mint, as a department of government, was able to claim Crown immunity, which meant that it could not be prosecuted, nor did it have to face a public hearing.

Facing charges

In 2002, Jairo Soto-Mendoza, a member of the Columbian diplomatic staff in London, was accused of murdering a man who had mugged his son. Mr Mendoza and his son reported the matter to the police and both volunteered an account of what had taken place. The Columbian government chose to set aside Mr Mendoza's diplomatic immunity and the case eventually came to court.

After listening to the evidence and discussing the evidence for four days, the jury returned a verdict of not guilty, and Mr Mendoza was released.

Equality

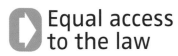

Equal access to the law

For everyone to stand a fair chance of having an equal hearing in court there needs to be a way of helping those who could not normally afford the cost of a lawyer to advise and represent them.

Legal costs

When a person asks a lawyer for legal advice, or needs a solicitor or barrister to act for them, there are almost always fees or costs to be paid. These can be very high. Therefore, if a legal system is to be fair and provide justice for everyone, there needs to be some way in which people can be helped with the financial costs of their case. Otherwise many will be unable to take legal action or be properly represented in court.

The importance of this idea in criminal cases is recognised in the European Convention on Human Rights. Article 6 states that free legal assistance should be given to someone charged with a criminal offence if they do not have the means to pay and "the interests of justice so require", see also page 134.

Legal aid

Until shortly after the Second World War, many people in Britain had to rely on charity if they were ever to take a case to court. The cost of getting help and advice from a solicitor or barrister was beyond the reach of most people, and many lawyers worked voluntarily to help and advise the poor.

In 1949, the government introduced a scheme by which fees were paid to lawyers to provide legal services to the poor and those who were not particularly well-off. This was known as

legal aid. It was originally seen as part of the welfare state and was available to about 80 per cent of the population. At first, the scheme applied only to civil cases, but during the 1960s and 70s was widened to include criminal trials as well.

By the mid 1980s the bill for legal aid had become very high, and each government since then has looked for ways of reducing this. Today, far fewer people are entitled to help from the state with legal costs – particularly in civil cases – than they once were.

Criminal legal aid

The consequences of someone having a criminal conviction can be very serious. A person in this position risks losing their reputation, their job, and sometimes their liberty. It is therefore in the interests of justice that people have help and advice in presenting their case in court – particularly because they will be up against the powerful machinery of the state.

In almost all circumstances, anyone who is arrested, or who goes to a police station voluntarily, is entitled to legal advice from the solicitor on duty, or from a solicitor of their choice. The consultation with the duty solicitor is free.

Anyone charged and sent to trial may also be eligible for help with the cost of a solicitor or barrister to represent them in court. This is traditionally known as legal aid, although *representation order* is the term used today.

A representation order will be granted if:

- **a conviction would have a serious effect on the life of the defendant, or**
- **the proceedings in court are likely to be difficult for the accused to understand, or**
- **the case involves an important question of law, or**
- **a lawyer is needed to protect a witness against cross-examination by the accused.**

Controversial

In 2005, Bolton Wanderer's footballer, El-Hadji Diouf from Senegal, was accused of spitting at a fan during a match against Middlesbrough. He was charged with disorderly conduct and granted legal aid – despite his reportedly high earnings of £40,000 a week.

Many people voiced disapproval of his legal costs being paid by the state. But a spokeswoman explained that the footballer had been granted legal aid for two reasons. Firstly, as a French speaker, he would have difficulty in defending himself. Secondly, if convicted, he was likely to be given a football banning order, which would put him out of work.

Civil legal aid

The government body with responsibility for trying to ensure that people get the help and advice they need in civil cases is called the Community Legal Service. It provides funds for advice centres like the CAB (Citizens Advice Bureau) and Law Centres, and supports a network of solicitors who can provide clients with help and advice and sometimes represent them in court.

Publicly-funded help from a solicitor, however, is generally available only to someone on a low income or with a relatively small amount of savings. It is available for many types of cases, but not for those involving personal injury. A person who is injured at work or in a road accident is most unlikely to receive public funds to pay for a solicitor to present their case in court. In cases of this kind, the person taking the case will normally agree to pay the solicitor a fixed sum for the cost of the case, plus an extra amount if the result is successful. (This is known as a conditional fee arrangement, or sometimes, no-win, no-fee.)

Equality

Freedom from discrimination

Traditionally, the law in Britain has emphasised personal liberty and the right of people to employ, trade with, or let accommodation to whoever they want. However, the freedom for people to do this can make the lives of many others very difficult – denying them opportunities to work and have an equal standard of living. In the 1950s and 60s it was not uncommon to see signs for rooms saying, "No coloureds, no Irish" and for women to be excluded from many areas of work. For this reason, Parliament eventually decided to intervene and create new laws to forbid certain kinds of discrimination.

Racial discrimination

The first UK law protecting people from racial discrimination was passed in 1965. It prohibited racial discrimination in public places, like bars, restaurants and hotels, and on public transport – but did not make it illegal to discriminate in employment or housing. By 1976, the law had been extended to cover both these areas. In addition, people who believed they had suffered racial discrimination at work were given the right to take their case to an employment tribunal and obtain compensation for the losses and damage they had suffered.

During the 1980s and 90s, further laws were passed making it an offence to stir up racial hatred, or use racist language in public in a way that causes harassment or alarm. Courts also became required to punish more severely offenders whose crimes were shown to have a racial motive.

Anyone taking a case of racial discrimination to an employment tribunal needs to show that they have been treated less favourably than another because of their race, colour, ethnic group, or nationality.

Sometimes it can be difficult for a person to prove this, particularly against a company or large organisation. In order to minimise this difficulty, once a reasonable case has been made that discrimination took place, it is then up to the company or organisation charged with discrimination to show that they did not act in an unlawful way. This is the opposite of the procedure followed in criminal cases, where the requirement is for the prosecution to prove the guilt of the accused, rather than the defendant having to prove their innocence.

Racist abuse

In 2005, an army staff sergeant was awarded £171,000 in compensation after suffering racist taunts from other soldiers, including a senior officer, over a prolonged period of time. The sergeant had been repeatedly insulted, with words such as 'nigger', and had been the subject of a mock job application in which he was given the identity of a character with learning difficulties. On the same form, the section on nationality had been completed with the word "British", followed by six question marks. The ordeal had a serious effect on the sergeant's health and he left the Army after more than 20 years' service.

The case of Stephen Lawrence

Stephen Lawrence was a young black man of 18 who was attacked and killed as he waited with his friend to catch a bus in Eltham, south east London. The events of the night in 1993 are remembered not only because of a man's death, but also because the people who are responsible have never been brought to justice.

Numerous mistakes by the police during the investigation gave rise to a special enquiry, headed by retired High Court judge, Sir William Macpherson. Sir William's report strongly criticised the police for the way in which they had handled the investigation; for example, by failing to keep proper records, not pursuing suspects, and treating Stephen Lawrence's family in an insensitive and patronising manner.

The report stated that many of the shortcomings were a result of the police investigating a crime in which the victim was a black person. Had the victim been white, the report stated, most of the failures would probably not have occurred. This is an example of what is called institutional racism – a failure of an organisation to provide a proper service to people because of their colour, culture, ethnic origin or nationality.

A duty to promote good relations

Partly as a result of the institutional racism highlighted by the Stephen Lawrence Inquiry, changes in the law now make it unlawful for public authorities – such as government departments, schools, the police, and the prison service – to do anything that constitutes racial discrimination.

Public authorities also have a legal duty to promote good relations between racial groups. Anyone who believes they have suffered racial discrimination by a public authority has the right to bring their complaint to a court.

Sexual discrimination

For many years, the law gave employers and husbands almost absolute freedom to discriminate against women. Until 1839, a woman had no right to keep her child if she and her husband separated. A married woman had no right to own property until 1882, and it was only in 1891 that the High Court decided that a husband had no right to imprison his wife in order to ensure that she had sex with him.

Today, the *Equal Pay Act 1970* and *Sex Discrimination Act 1975* make it unlawful to discriminate on grounds of sex in employment, education, housing, or in providing goods and services. It is also unlawful to discriminate at work or in job adverts against someone who is married.

Taking action

Sex discrimination laws work in a similar way to those prohibiting racial discrimination. A person who believes that they are a victim of sexual discrimination may take their complaint to an employment tribunal and once again the main burden of proof is on the defendant.

Equality

Disability discrimination

Legislation giving disabled people rights of equality was passed by Parliament in 1995. It is against the law to discriminate against a disabled person in employment, education, when renting or selling property, or over access to services, like shops or restaurants. It is also unlawful for a disabled person at work to be harassed or have jokes made about their disability.

Without good reason

A Sheffield taxi driver was fined £150 for refusing to carry a blind woman with her guide dog. The woman complained to the council who traced the driver and took him to court. Under the _Town Police Clauses Act 1847_, it is an offence for the driver of a licensed taxi or hire care to refuse to take a passenger, without good reason.

Employers are required to make reasonable adjustments to the working environment, to enable or to allow a disabled person to work. A disabled person may be refused work only if the employer can show that they have a sufficiently good reason for doing so, and that the problem can't be overcome by making reasonable adjustments to the workplace.

Other discrimination

Legal protection has recently been given against two further areas of discrimination. In December 2003, it became against the law to discriminate against someone at work either because of their religion or their sexuality – but the regulations do not extend to housing, education or the supply of goods and services.

New regulations against age discrimination come into force in October 2006.

Promoting equality

There are currently three separate official organisations with responsibility for tackling discrimination. The Commission for Racial Equality, **www.cre.gov.uk** helps people with complaints about racial discrimination. The Equal Opportunities Commission, **www.eoc.gov.uk** deals with sex discrimination and the Disability Rights Commission, **www.grc-gb.org** helps people suffering discrimination because of their disability.

In 2007, the government plans to merge these into a single organisation, the Commission for Equality and Human Rights.

GOVERNMENT

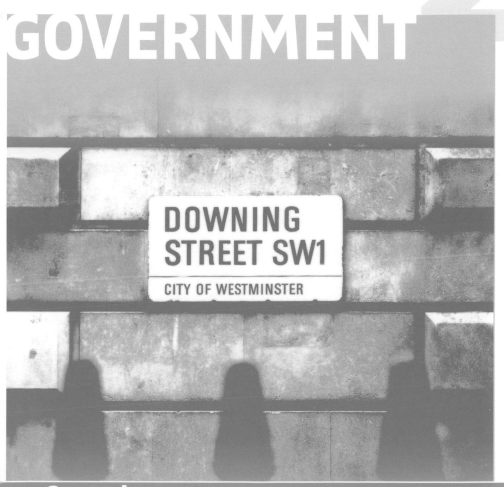

DOWNING
STREET SW1

CITY OF WESTMINSTER

Central government

GOVERNING BRITAIN

There are few areas of public, and even personal, life in Britain today with which the government has no concern.

Until the middle of the nineteenth century, governments tended to deal mainly with foreign affairs, law and order, defence, and trade. This began to change during industrialisation. As towns and cities grew in size, the government also became involved in improving people's living and working conditions.

Today, government is expected to manage a wide range of social issues, including employment, health, education, housing and the environment, as well as the economy, foreign affairs and law and order.

Under the UK constitution, a government has extensive powers with which to carry out this range of tasks.

Government powers

In theory, a government may take any action that it wishes, even one that is widely unpopular, as long as it remains within the law. It need not consult or take into account the views of any group or individual.

However, a government that constantly ignores the views of the people it governs is likely to lose its authority, even if its actions are within the law.

Anti-war

A crowd of about a million people marched through central London in February 2003 to protest against the government's decision to go to war with Iraq. There were similar, smaller, protests in many other towns and cities in the UK. In spite of this opposition the government refused to change its policy.

Riots

In 1990, the government introduced a new tax to pay for local government services. It was known as the poll tax, and required most people – whatever their income – to pay the same amount for local services.

Although there were some reductions for the poor, the tax was very unpopular and there was widespread protest. Some people refused to pay and a public demonstration in London turned into a riot. Later in the year, the Prime Minister Margaret Thatcher resigned – partly because of the unpopularity of this tax. Soon afterwards the poll tax was withdrawn, and the council tax introduced in its place.

Central government

Where does the government get its power?

Most of the powers of a government are granted by Parliament.

Parliament

Parliament, which represents the people of the UK, passes laws that allow, or authorise, a government to carry out its policies. Members of the government, that is ministers, have to answer to Parliament for their decisions.

If a government loses the confidence of the House of Commons, it can not continue in office.

The Crown

Until the seventeenth century, the king or queen had wide powers to govern the country. They had the right – known as a prerogative – to use these powers almost without the control of either Parliament or the courts.

Over the years, most of these powers – such as the power to make laws – have been transferred to Parliament, but others are now held by the government. They are still known as the Crown or Royal Prerogative, even though they are no longer in the hands of the monarch. Under the Crown or Royal Prerogative a government has the right to:

- **declare war and send troops abroad,**
- **make international and European treaties,**
- **make appointments and award honours,**
- **make major changes to the way that it works.**

No confidence

In 1979, members of the House of Commons passed a vote of no confidence in the Labour government, led by the Prime Minister, James Callaghan. As a result, Mr Callaghan was forced to ask the Queen to dissolve Parliament and to hold a general election. Labour lost the election, and a new government was formed, under the leadership of Margaret Thatcher.

Strictly speaking, the government does not need to consult Parliament about any of these actions, although it did do so before the Iraq War in 2003. Some people ask whether this should be made compulsory. But on the other hand, the use of the Royal Prerogative enables a government to react quickly to new and possibly dangerous circumstances.

War

The Royal Prerogative enables a government to send troops into action without consulting Parliament.

In 1982 the government sent a military force to relieve the Falkland Islands, which had been invaded by Argentina. The Leader of the Opposition argued that the House of Commons had the right to discuss this before any action was taken. The Prime Minister, Margaret Thatcher, disagreed. It was the right of the government, she said, to negotiate and make decisions, which the House of Commons could pass judgement on afterwards.

Central government

The Prime Minister

Like much of the British constitution the position of Prime Minister is one that has evolved through history. Today it is agreed that Britain's first Prime Minister was Sir Robert Walpole, who held the position of First Lord of the Treasury from 1721. This is still the official title held by the Prime Minister today. The role and powers of the post are governed largely by convention, not by law.

Why 'Prime' Minister?

Sir Robert Walpole was a member of the Cabinet that advised George I, who became king in 1714. George, who was German by birth, spoke poor English and had little interest in British politics. As a result, he relied on Walpole and the Cabinet to help him rule the country.

To begin with, all members of the Cabinet were considered to be equal but Walpole made the position of First Lord of the Treasury the most important, or the 'first among equals'. The Latin phrase for this is *primus inter pares* and from this comes the term Prime Minister.

Appointment

It is a firm convention that the Prime Minister should be a member of the House of Commons, and may only be appointed by the queen or king.

Party leader

Although the monarch could appoint any MP as Prime Minister, in practice it is always the leader of the political party with most seats in the House of Commons.

Sometimes a political party changes its leader whilst in government. As a result, there will be a new Prime Minister – without people in the country as a whole having any say in the matter.

Change at the top

Prime Minister Margaret Thatcher resigned as leader of the Conservatives in 1990 after losing the support of her party. John Major was elected as new leader by the 372 Conservative MPs, and became the new British Prime Minister.

Crisis?

If a general election (see page 126) does not result in a clear majority for one party in the House of Commons (called a 'hung' parliament), the queen or king may have to make a choice about who to ask to form a government and become Prime Minister.

In this situation the monarch has a clear constitutional responsibility to be politically impartial. Normally an outgoing Prime Minister is asked to advise on who will take their place, but the monarch does not have to take this advice.

The role of the Prime Minister

There are a large number of responsibilities attached to the office of Prime Minister. Some of the most important are described below.

Government appointments

The Prime Minister, on behalf of the queen or king, appoints (and dismisses) the other members of the government. By law, no more than 95 people are entitled to receive the salary payable to a member of the government.

Other appointments

The Prime Minister, as leader of the government, recommends a wide range of other appointments that are made by the queen or king. The power to do this – known as patronage – is one of the Prime Minister's most important powers.

The Prime Minister recommends to the queen or king names for appointment to senior positions of the armed forces and security services, the Church of England, the judiciary (see page 134) and the heads of important public bodies, such as the BBC. The Prime Minister also proposes names to the monarch for the granting of life peerages (see page 132), knighthoods and other honours. By convention, the monarch is expected to agree to the Prime Minister's nominations.

In the past there were few restrictions on the names put forward by the Prime Minster. Recently there have been moves to make the system more open and accountable (see Judicial appointments, page 143).

The Lavender List

By convention, retiring Prime Ministers may recommend honours for those people who have worked for them during their term of office.

When Harold Wilson resigned as Prime Minister in 1976, his list of nominations caused some controversy. The Lavender List, as it became known, was written on lavender coloured paper by Mr Wilson's personal secretary, Marcia Williams. Many believed that some of the names on the list were designed to reward political and personal favours. They included Mrs Williams' own honour as Lady Falkender, and also the name of Joseph Kagan, whose firm made a particular type of raincoat that Mr Wilson wore, and who was later imprisoned for false accounting.

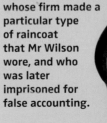

Central government

The Civil Service

The leader of the government is also the minister in charge of the Civil Service, see page 83. He or she is responsible for the appointment of senior civil servants and for the efficient and effective working of the service.

In Parliament

The Prime Minister, as leader of the government is accountable to Parliament for the actions of the government as a whole. Each Wednesday, when Parliament is in session, the Prime Minister attends the House of Commons to answer questions from MPs.

At the Palace

The Prime Minister is responsible for dealing with any serious or sensitive matters that involve the queen or king or the royal family. He or she has a duty to keep the Queen in touch with the actions of her government. There is a regular meeting between the Queen and the Prime Minister each Tuesday evening.

The use of armed forces

As leader of the government, the Prime Minister has the ultimate say in how Britain's armed forces are used. He or she is also the government minister in charge of Britain's intelligence and security services. Only the Prime Minister can activate the codes that would launch Britain's nuclear strike force.

Representing Britain

It is the Prime Minister's task to represent the UK at important international conferences, such as the European Council or United Nations, see page 104. It is normally the Prime Minister or the Foreign Secretary who signs international treaties and agreements on behalf of the UK government.

The powers of the Prime Minister

The Prime Minister has a range of powers that enable him or her to carry out their duties. A number of these come from the fact that it is the Prime Minister who has most control over the Crown or Royal Prerogative.

Control of the government

The fact that a Prime Minister appoints and dismisses members of the government, gives him or her a great deal of power over the conduct of government business and policy.

A Prime Minister has authority over the Cabinet (see page 80), chairing its meetings and deciding the agenda, and has great influence on the discussions of Cabinet committees.

Control of Parliament

Although, by law, there must be a general election at least every five years (see page 126), it is the Prime Minister alone who has the power to ask the monarch to dissolve Parliament and call an early election.

This right means that a Prime Minister can time an election to gain maximum advantage from political or economic circumstances and so have a better chance of remaining in power.

Misjudgement?

Sometimes this decision can backfire. James Callaghan delayed calling an election in 1978, when many think he would have been re-elected as Prime Minister. Instead, the election took place the following year, during a period of economic unrest. The government was very unpopular and Mr Callaghan was defeated by Margaret Thatcher.

Government ministers, under the leadership of the Prime Minister, have a great deal of control over the time allowed in Parliament for debate on policies and proposals for new law.

A varied position

The UK constitution does not set out clearly either the powers available to the Prime Minister, or the limits to those powers. This means that the position of Prime Minister is flexible, depending on the circumstances, their political ideals and character.

The position of Prime Minister has become steadily more important and powerful over time. Some argue that this has gone too far while others believe that collective discussion of senior ministers and the Cabinet continues to be important.

Central government

The Cabinet

The place of the Cabinet in British government goes back over 300 years to the time when advisors to King William III met separately to hold discussions in a small private room. This room was called a 'cabinet' and this word came to be used to describe the group of the closest advisors to the monarch, not the room itself.

Today the Cabinet is made up of about 20 senior ministers, all chosen by the Prime Minister. It is the core of government, and the place where final decisions about important areas of government policy are usually made.

Membership

There are no restrictions on the size of the Cabinet. Since the Second World War, it has varied between 16 and 24 members. The Prime Minister must select members of the Cabinet from the House of Commons or the House of Lords. In practice, almost all of them are from the Commons.

Holders of major government positions, such as the Chancellor of the Exchequer, the Home Secretary and the Foreign Secretary, always have a seat in the Cabinet. The remaining members are heads of other government departments or those with the task of managing the government's business in Parliament. These include the Leader of the House of Commons and the Chief Whip (see page 124). Membership of the current Cabinet can be found at **www.number10.gov.uk**.

Meetings

Whilst Parliament is in session, the Cabinet generally meets weekly. However, it can meet as often as necessary, particularly during a crisis.

Discussions in Cabinet are held in secret and, both by convention and under the *Official Secrets Act*, ministers are not allowed to reveal what was discussed. In fact, records of Cabinet meetings are not released for 30 years, and some information that the government considers particularly sensitive, may be kept secret for even longer. See also **Freedom of information**, page 51.

Cabinet Secretary

As the business of government has become more complex, the Cabinet has become more organised. In 1916 the first Cabinet Secretary was appointed, to keep minutes of all meetings and record decisions. Today the holder of this office is the most senior civil servant, responsible only to the Prime Minister. It is a powerful and influential position.

The role of the Cabinet

It is very difficult to define the role of the Cabinet precisely, since there are no formal written rules laying this out. The way in which any Cabinet operates also depends on the political circumstances of the time, including the strength of the governing party, and on the personalities of senior ministers, particularly the Prime Minister.

Making decisions
One accepted role of the Cabinet is to consider major questions of policy or issues of great public importance. On occasions, such as a national crisis or strong disagreement between different departments or ministers, the full Cabinet may be called upon to make decisions. In practice, this rarely happens, since key decisions are normally taken by the Prime Minister and smaller groups of the most important ministers and advisors.

Approving decisions
The Cabinet has an important role in approving decisions that are made elsewhere within the government. The Cabinet receives reports and recommendations from Cabinet committees that must be approved before they can be put into practice. The Cabinet will normally need to approve major policy decisions taken by the Prime Minister.

A check to the power of the Prime Minister
As Cabinet approval is needed for major government decisions, it would be very difficult for a Prime Minister to ignore its opinion continuously. Although the wishes of a Prime Minister will generally be accepted; if he or she consistently acts without the support of Cabinet colleagues they will eventually be unable to maintain their position.

Some Prime Ministers, like Margaret Thatcher and Tony Blair, have preferred to operate beyond the traditional structure of Cabinet decision-making. However, periods of unpopularity or a poor election showing can force a Prime Minister to consult his or her Cabinet colleagues more often.

Not accepted
In 1979, the Cabinet at first rejected Margaret Thatcher's ideas for the reform of trade unions. In 1998, proposals to alter the welfare system put forward by Frank Field, minister for welfare reform, were turned down by Tony Blair's Cabinet.

Central government

Collective responsibility

Members of the Cabinet must follow the convention of collective responsibility. This means that all members of the Cabinet must agree publicly with all Cabinet or Cabinet committee decisions, whatever their private opinion. Any member of the Cabinet who is unable to do this must either resign from the Cabinet, or face dismissal. The purpose of this convention is to allow full and frank discussion in private, while still allowing the government to appear united and jointly responsible for its decisions.

Collective responsibility is an important way of maintaining the authority and unity of the government. It is never formally questioned, though it may be weakened at times.

Resignation

In 2003, Robin Cook, then Leader of the House, resigned from his position in the Cabinet. He disagreed so strongly with the government's decision to go to war against Iraq that he was not able to support it in public.

One of his main concerns was that Britain was acting without the agreement of international bodies like the United Nations and European Union, saying in his speech to the House of Commons, "neither the international community nor the British public is persuaded that there is an urgent and compelling reason for this military action in Iraq".

Cabinet committees

To allow the Cabinet to operate more effectively, much of its work is carried out by committees.

Permanent committees

Most of these are permanent, or standing committees that are set up for the life of a government to consider major areas of policy, such as energy or the environment. Details of the current standing committees can be found at **www.cabinetoffice.gov.uk**.

Special or 'ad hoc' committees

In times of war, or other national emergencies, a small group of Cabinet members is normally formed to take quick decisions and supervise government action.

'War Cabinet'

During the Falklands War in 1982, the Prime Minister, Margaret Thatcher, set up a small 'War Cabinet' to oversee military operations. More recent examples of special committees include those set up to look at the financing of the new Wembley Stadium, and at the work of animal rights' activists.

The Prime Minister decides the number, focus, and membership of all Cabinet committees, and will chair the most important. Reports from the committees are presented to the full Cabinet for discussion or agreement. Where members of a committee cannot agree over a decision themselves, the matter may be referred to the full Cabinet.

 The Civil Service

The Civil Service was originally the name given to the group of servants to the king or queen that kept accounts and administered the kingdom. This was in contrast to those in military service who defended the kingdom.

Today the Civil Service does far more than keep a government's accounts. Its task is to help the elected government to formulate policies, to carry out its decisions, and to administer public services.

Background

Each major department of government has a staff of civil servants, headed by a permanent secretary, who is responsible to the political minister in charge of the department. The staff provide information and advice to help the minister decide on policy and will then ensure that this policy is put into practice. Today, as well as administrators, the Civil Service includes scientists, lawyers, medical officers, accountants and many other professions.

In Britain today there are about 500,000 civil servants. While most of these work in providing services directly to the public, such as running employment services or staffing prisons, there is a small

group who are members of the Senior Civil Service. This elite, often called 'mandarins', has a powerful and important role in governing the country.

Neutrality

Under the British constitution, civil servants do not work for the government itself, but are 'servants of the Crown', see page 91. This means that they are expected to be politically *neutral*, loyally serving the government of the day – whether or not they agree with its political ideas.

When a government is defeated in a general election, the Civil Service must immediately transfer its loyalty to the new government, even if this means a complete reversal of its position.

In order to bring about this change, it is now an established convention that shadow ministers (see page 124) meet with senior civil servants before an election, so that plans can be prepared for a new government. Conservative Prime Minister John Major allowed civil servants to meet with opposition Labour party officials for more than a year before the election in 1997.

Special advisers
Government ministers also receive help from special advisers. These may do a range of jobs including: giving expert advice, writing the minister's speeches, or helping a minister with the presentation of their policy. Unlike civil servants, special advisers do not have to be politically neutral.

Central government

Permanence

Unlike a number of other countries, such as the United States, senior civil servants in Britain are appointed to permanent positions and do not lose their jobs when there is a new government.

It is argued that this permanence helps to make sure that governments have the support of an experienced Civil Service, and that civil servants themselves remain politically neutral.

A 'closed' service

Margaret Thatcher, however, believed that the permanence of senior civil servants made them resistant to change and less efficient. While she was Prime Minister she set up a thorough review of the way in which the Civil Service operated. The result was a range of reforms that changed the structure of the Civil Service and has reduced its numbers by about a third since 1979.

Change

In an effort to improve efficiency and deliver better public services, recent governments have changed the way the Civil Service works. Although each department is still run by a core of civil servants directly accountable to ministers, many tasks are now carried out by non-governmental bodies like the Driving Standards Agency and Prison Service.

These organisations are each headed by a chief executive or director general who is answerable to a minister, but responsible for the operations of their agency and staff. This may lead to disagreements between a minister and a director over who has control over certain decisions.

Conflict

In 1994, six high-risk prisoners escaped from Whitemoor Prison in Cambridgeshire. When the report of the enquiry into the break-out was published, the Home Secretary, Michael Howard, instructed Derek Lewis, the Director of the Prison Service, to dismiss the governor of Whitemoor Prison.

Mr Lewis refused, insisting that he had full confidence in the governor, and that a decision of this kind was not the Minister's responsibility. Mr Howard disagreed, and went on to dismiss Mr Lewis, as well as the Prison governor. Mr Lewis later won compensation for wrongful dismissal.

Confidentiality

Much of the advice that civil servants provide for a government is confidential. All civil servants must sign the *Official Secrets Act*, under which it a criminal offence for a civil servant to pass on any official information, even when they leave or retire from the service. In return, government ministers are expected not to reveal the names or the nature of the advice they receive from their civil servants.

Occasionally civil servants decide to bring a government's action to public attention.

About turn

In 1982, during the Falklands War, an Argentine cruiser, the *General Belgrano*, was torpedoed by a British submarine, and 323 people lost their lives. The large number of casualties led many people to ask whether the attack should have taken place.

At the time of the sinking, the government stated that the warship had been sailing towards British forces, threatening British lives. However, soon afterwards it was realised that this had been a mistake and that the *Belgrano* had been sailing in the *opposite* direction, away from the British fleet. No attempt was made by the government to correct this mistake.

Clive Ponting, a senior civil servant at the Ministry of Defence, believed that the government should have set the record straight, and decided to pass documents giving the true picture to MP, Tam Dalyell. Mr Ponting was charged, under the *Official Secrets Act*, with communicating information to an unauthorised person.

In his defence, Clive Ponting claimed that he had released the documents in the public interest. The judge instructed the jury to find Mr Ponting guilty. They did not, and he was released.

Central government

 ## Control over government

Although a government has wide powers at its disposal there are various mechanisms and institutions to ensure that it can be challenged if it tries to abuse its powers.

Parliament

Parliament has an important role in examining the work of the government, see page 120. Members of both Houses debate government policy and carefully check its proposals for new law. The government has to state that each proposed new law is compatible with the *Human Rights Act 1998* or take special steps to justify not complying with it. These measures are carefully scrutinised.

The power of Parliament to control a government depends considerably on the size of the government majority in the House of Commons. Parliament has little power to check a government with a substantial majority, such as happened in 1983, when the Conservative Party had a majority of 144 seats, or in 2001, with a Labour majority of 167.

At such times the role of the House of Lords, where there is now no overall majority for any party, can become more significant in objecting to government proposals. However the power of a government in the House of Commons will still enable it to pass almost any measure that it wishes (see **Parliament Acts**, page 131).

A minister's responsibility

All ministers are responsible to Parliament for their actions as head of their department, and for those of their officials. Each minister must attend Parliament regularly to answer questions face to face. He or she is also required to answer written questions from members of both the House of Commons and the House of Lords.

Ministers must tell the truth. The charge of lying to Parliament is very serious, and a minister found to have done so may have to resign.

Ministers are legally responsible for every act of government in which they take part, and may be challenged in the court over whether they have acted in accordance with the law. This is known as a judicial review, see pages 87 and 144.

Ministerial code
Since 1945 a set of rules have been developed to guide ministers in the conduct of their public duties. These rules are published as the Ministerial Code. Failure to observe these rules may result in a minister being dismissed.

Judicial review

A judicial review is a court proceeding in which a judge, or panel of judges considers whether the government has acted within the law. Judicial reviews of government action have become more common during the last 40 years as governments become involved in a wider range of activity.

A judicial review may examine whether the government has acted within the powers granted to it by an Act of Parliament. If the court rules that it has acted outside its powers, the government must withdraw its proposal. A judicial review may also examine whether a government has acted in the way that the law as passed by Parliament intended, see also page 144.

Watchdogs

A number of independent watchdogs have been established that have an important role in ensuring that the government uses its powers fairly and properly. These include organisations such as the Committee on Standards in Public Life, the Audit Commission, and the Parliamentary Ombudsman.

The electorate

The clearest restriction to the power of any government is that it must face an election at least every five years, see page 126. If a government loses the support of the electorate as shown in a general election, then it has no authority to govern and is replaced. Although a government has very wide powers, ultimately it can only use these whilst it has the support of the people.

Gobbledegook

A survey by the National Audit Office, which checks on the efficiency of government departments, revealed that in 2005 the Department for Work and Pensions (DWP) spent £31m publishing 250 different information leaflets. The Audit Office said that the leaflets were often out of date and difficult for the public to understand.

The DWP was urged to cut the number of leaflets it produced, to make them easier to understand and to make sure that people can get hold of information when it is required.

Central government

 The monarchy

The United Kingdom is a constitutional monarchy. This means that although the queen or king is head of state, they no longer have any political power. They reign – but do not rule.

Until the end of the seventeenth century the power to govern Britain lay with the monarch. He or she could pass laws, decide that the country should go to war and, with Parliament's permission, raise taxes. Important changes in 1689 and 1701 meant that much of this power was passed to Parliament.

Since then, Parliament has steadily grown in power and the role of the queen or king is now very limited. All the functions still performed by the British monarch are governed by convention – unwritten rules that have been established as the power of the monarchy gradually disappeared.

The role of the monarch

By convention, the queen or king acts only on the advice of government ministers and must remain outside party politics. In return, politicians are usually very careful to respect this neutrality, and not to draw the monarch into political controversy. The main functions of the monarch today are listed below.

The dissolution of Parliament

This is the official term for bringing a Parliament to an end, so that a general election can take place. Only the king or queen may dissolve Parliament, although this is normally on the advice of the Prime Minister, and it is one of the most important powers still held by the monarch. The last time that the queen or king went to Parliament to carry this out *in person* was in 1818.

When the Prime Minister decides to call a general election today, he or she goes to Buckingham Palace and formally asks the queen or king to issue a proclamation for Parliament to be dissolved.

Not tested

Although it has not been used in modern times, the monarch still has the right to refuse to dissolve Parliament. This would only happen if the queen or king judged that it was not in the national interest to do so – for example, if a Prime Minister wanted to call an election just to boost his or her own position.

The royal assent

Before a Bill can pass into law as an Act of Parliament, it requires the approval, or assent, of the monarch. The last monarch to refuse to approve an Act was Queen Anne in 1707.

Today, assent is not reported to Parliament by the monarch in person. The last monarch to give her assent in person was Queen Victoria in 1854.

Appointing the Prime Minister

The monarch alone has the power to appoint the Prime Minister. However she or he must choose as Prime Minister someone who will have the support of a majority of MPs in the House of Commons. Normally the leader of the party with the largest number of seats in the House of Commons is invited to form a government.

'Hung parliament'

If no party has an outright majority of MPs, it is called a 'hung parliament'. On such occasions, the role of the queen or king in asking someone to become Prime Minister and form a government becomes more significant.

In these circumstances, the monarch waits to see if the serving Prime Minister can form a government with support from other parties. If not, the Prime Minister must resign – he or she cannot call another general election – and the leader of the main opposition party is then asked to form a government.

This situation seldom occurs as the voting system used in the UK (see page 128) almost always results in a clear majority for one party.

Two elections

The general election of February 1974 produced no clear winner. Neither the Conservative Party, led by the Prime Minister Edward Heath, nor the Labour Party, under Harold Wilson, had an outright majority of seats in the House of Commons.

Mr Heath tried to form a government with the third largest party, the Liberals, but this proved impossible. He was advised that, in these circumstances, the Queen would not agree to dissolve Parliament for another general election. As a result, Mr Heath resigned as Prime Minister.

The Queen then asked Mr Wilson to become Prime Minister, and he became leader of a minority government (that is, one without a majority of seats in the House of Commons). In October 1974, Mr Wilson asked the Queen to dissolve Parliament for another general election, which he won with a small majority.

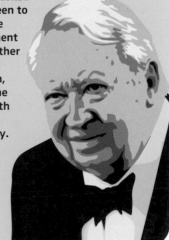

Central government

Other government ministers

In practice the Prime Minister now appoints all other government ministers. However, as Ministers of the Crown they are officially appointed by the monarch, and receive their royal seals of office on appointment.

Rights

The monarch has the right and duty to "advise, to warn and to encourage" the government. This summary of the relationship between the monarch and the government was written during Queen Victoria's reign but still holds true today. The queen or king has the right to see Cabinet papers but cannot dictate government policy and must abide by the advice of her or his ministers.

Each week the Queen holds an audience with the Prime Minister. The content of these meetings, and all communication between her and her government, remains strictly confidential.

The Queen and Parliament

Officially, Parliament is made up of the House of Commons, the House of Lords, and the Crown. Its formal title is the Queen (or King) in Parliament.

The State Opening

The position of the Queen in Parliament is most obvious at the annual State Opening, when the Queen goes to Westminster in person to open a new session of Parliament. This formal, ceremonial and public occasion, is one of the few on which the Queen wears a crown and robes. At the opening the Queen addresses a speech to both Houses of Parliament from her throne in the House of Lords.

The Queen's Speech

This speech, written by the government, is read by the Queen at the State Opening. It outlines the government's policy for the coming session of Parliament, and sets out the new laws it intends to create. The Houses of Parliament can not start their public business until the speech has been read.

Elections

As head of state, the Queen must be politically neutral. It is considered unconstitutional for the monarch or their heirs to take part in any way in local, national, or European elections, although the law does not actually prohibit this.

The Head of the Church of England

The monarch is also the Supreme Governor of the Church of England.

Although the Church of England has little political power today, it remains the "established" national religion in England, giving it special privileges, like the 26 seats in the House of Lords reserved for the most senior Anglican bishops. It also means that laws of the Church of England are approved by Parliament.

Honours and appointments

In the past an important way for a king or queen to maintain their power was by granting people land, titles, money or jobs. Today it is the government that grants honours and makes appointments to public bodies, universities, the Church or the military. However, these must still be formally approved by the king or queen.

The monarch may award some honours independently of the government. The most important of these are the Order of the Garter, the Order of the Thistle, and the Order of Merit.

Order of the Garter

The Order of the Garter is the most senior and the oldest British Order of Chivalry, and was founded by Edward III in 1348. The Order, consisting of the King and twenty-five knights, was intended by Edward III to be the highest reward for loyalty and for military merit. Today Knights of the Garter are chosen personally by the Queen to honour those people who have held public office, who have contributed in a particular way to national life, or who have served her personally.

Royal finance

The costs of the monarchy are covered by Parliament in a grant called the Civil List. In 2000, the annual amount of the Civil List for the next ten years was set at £7.9 million per year.

The Queen personally owns two palaces, at Balmoral and Sandringham, but the other royal palaces are maintained at the country's expense. Further funds are provided for official transport.

Tax

Since 1993 the Queen and her heir, the Prince of Wales, have chosen to pay council tax, and income tax on their private income, though the law does not require this.

The Crown

Although the Queen today has very little power herself, the position she holds, known as the Crown, remains an important part of the UK constitution.

The Crown is the term used for the office and authority of the state, as opposed to the individual person who is king or queen. It is a reminder of the fact that monarchs used to have considerable personal power.

The use of the term Crown to describe state authority can be widely seen. For example, government ministers are officially called 'Ministers of the Crown'. The judicial system (see page 134) is carried out in the name of the Crown by Her Majesty's judges. Ships of the Royal Navy are called Her Majesty's Ships (HMS) and members of the armed forces swear an oath of allegiance to the Crown.

Crown Prerogative

Although most of the powers once belonging to the monarch have now been passed to Parliament, some may be exercised by the government, particularly the Prime Minister, see page 74.

Beyond central government

DEVOLUTION, REGIONAL AND LOCAL GOVERNMENT

Since 1997, the British government has taken steps to transfer certain parts of government away from London to the UK's nations and regions. This is known as devolution.

Today there is a Parliament in Scotland and Assemblies in Wales and Northern Ireland. There is an elected mayor for London, and Assemblies have been proposed for the English regions.

Every part of Britain also has a local authority or council. Sometimes these are large – covering a whole county or city, but they can be much smaller, with responsibilities limited to those of a small or medium-sized town.

Devolution: Scotland, Wales and Northern Ireland

The first elections for the Scottish Parliament and Welsh Assembly took place in 1999, giving people in Scotland and Wales political control over some of the matters that affect their lives.

Northern Ireland also has its own Assembly, but this was suspended by the British government in 2002, following a dispute between two of the major political parties in Northern Ireland.

The making of the United Kingdom

England
Westminster became the permanent centre of the government of England about 800 years ago. Before then, the King needed to travel about the country to assert his authority, and government was carried out from wherever he happened to be.

By the middle of the 1200s, the Palace of Westminster (the site of the present Houses of Parliament) became the main residence for the monarch and the meeting place for Parliament.

Over the next 300 years, English kings gradually secured their control over the whole country and by the time of Henry VIII, there was a strong central government based in London.

Wales
From the time of William the Conqueror, much of south Wales was ruled by the English.

However it was not until the early 1300s that the whole of Wales was largely under English control.

In 1536, the King of England, Henry VIII, wanted to secure his rule over Wales so he insisted that the laws of England were imposed on Wales. In return, the Welsh were granted seats in the Parliament in Westminster, but the English language was made compulsory for all legal and official purposes.

Scotland
Although there was frequent warfare between the English and Scots during the thirteenth and fourteenth centuries, the English were not able to conquer or control Scotland. Scotland had its own monarchy and Church, and developed its own legal system and Parliament quite separately from England.

When Elizabeth I, Queen of England, died in 1603, she was succeeded by James VI, King of Scotland. Although England and Scotland now had the same King, the two countries did not join together. Each continued with its own Parliament, legal and religious systems.

It was not until 1707 that the two Parliaments of Scotland and England eventually joined together, creating the Parliament of Great Britain. There was one Parliament in Westminster for the two countries, but Scotland kept its own legal system and remained independent of the Church of England.

Beyond central government

Ireland

The government decided to unite Ireland with the mainland by passing the *Act of Union* in 1800. This established the 'United Kingdom of Great Britain and Ireland'. The Irish Parliament was abolished, but 100 MPs represented Ireland in the united Parliament in Westminster.

Many in Ireland resented this change and by the 1880s there was a strong movement by Nationalists for 'Home Rule' – a form of self-government for Ireland. Others (Unionists), equally strongly wanted to keep the Union with the rest of the United Kingdom. The dispute between these two groups led to armed conflict.

It proved impossible to solve the disagreement between the Nationalists and the Unionists and so, in 1922, Ireland was divided. In 1949, the southern part of Ireland became the independent republic of Eire. The region in the north has remained part of what is now called the United Kingdom of Great Britain and Northern Ireland.

Calls for change

For more than 70 years, groups in Wales and Scotland called for greater freedom from central government in London. This movement gained support during the 1980s and 90s. When a Labour government came to power in 1997, it promised to hold separate referendums for the people of Scotland and Wales on its proposals for how their countries should be governed.

Later that year, people in Scotland voted, by a large majority, to approve the government's proposals for a Scottish Parliament. A smaller majority in Wales voted for a Welsh assembly.

The Scottish Parliament

The *Scotland Act 1998* led to the establishment of the first Scottish Parliament since 1707.

Today there are 129 members of the Scottish Parliament (MSPs), elected by a system of proportional representation, see page 128. Elections must take place every four years. More information about the Scottish Parliament can be found at **www.scottish.parliament.uk**.

Passing laws

MSPs may debate any matter that they wish in Parliament, but may only make laws on certain issues. These are known as 'devolved matters' and include health, education, the environment, the police and the justice system. The *Scotland Act* lists certain 'reserved areas', such as defence, foreign affairs, taxation and social security that remain under the control of the UK Parliament.

No smoking

The Scottish Parliament approved a ban on smoking in bars, restaurants and all public places in June 2005. The law came into effect in March 2006, more than a year before a similar ban takes effect in England.

Finance
The Scottish Parliament has the legal power to make small changes in the rate of income tax that applies to people in Scotland. At the time of writing, this power has not yet been used.

The Scottish Executive
This is the name given to the devolved body that governs Scotland in all matters over which it has control.

The Executive is led by a First Minister, chosen by MSPs – and appointed by the Queen. As in Westminster, ministers (who are all MSPs) take responsibility for different areas of government, and are accountable to the Scottish Parliament. More information about the Scottish Executive can be found at **www.scotland.gov.uk**.

The National Assembly for Wales

Wales has had the same government and laws as England for nearly 500 years and so has developed less of a tradition of self-government. For this reason, when the Assembly was created in 1999, it was given fewer powers of self-government than Scotland.

The Assembly does not have power to pass its own laws, but does decide how laws passed by the Westminster Parliament should apply in Wales.

There are 60 members of the Welsh Assembly, known as AMs (Assembly Members), who are elected by proportional representation. Elections must take place every four years. AMs have the responsibility for deciding how laws affecting for example, education, health, transport and the environment are put into practice in the best interest of the people of Wales. Members may also propose laws for the UK Parliament to consider.

Top-up fees
In May 2005 the Welsh Assembly voted against the Westminster Parliament's decision to raise tuition fees for students in Wales. As a result, from 2006, Welsh students studying at universities in Wales will pay no more than £1,200 a year in fees, with the remainder paid by the Assembly government. (This compares with a figure of up to £3,000 payable by students in England.)

Welsh students studying elsewhere in the UK will also pay a reduced fee, if the course they are taking is not available at a Welsh university.

The Assembly elects a First Minister to serve as their leader. He or she then appoints ministers responsible for particular areas of policy, such as health or education. All ministers are accountable to the National Assembly. More information about the National Assembly for Wales can be found at **www.wales.gov.uk**.

Further change?
In January 2006, MPs in Parliament at Westminster debated the *Government of Wales Bill*. If it is passed, it will lead to greater powers for the Welsh Assembly, and will eventually allows AMs to make laws in areas for which they already have responsibility – such as health and education.

Beyond central government

The Northern Ireland Assembly

The Northern Ireland Assembly was established in 1998 after agreement had been reached between the governments of the United Kingdom, the Republic of Ireland and the organisations that had been involved in the unrest and violence. This took place shortly before Easter, on 10th April, and has become known as the Good Friday Agreement.

There are 108 members of the Northern Ireland Assembly, elected by proportional representation, see page 128. The Assembly has powers to decide on matters such as education, agriculture, health and the environment in Northern Ireland.

Under the Good Friday Agreement the important positions in the government of Northern Ireland are divided between the main parties in the Assembly. For example the First Minister and the Deputy First Minister must be from different political parties.

The Assembly meets at Stormont, a large building on the outskirts of Belfast, and the site of the first Northern Ireland Parliament. The Parliament was stripped of its power in 1972 by British Prime Minister Edward Heath as the violence between the mainly Catholic Nationalist and Protestant Unionist communities worsened.

Argument

On 14th October 2002, UK Northern Ireland Minister John Reid, announced the immediate suspension of the Northern Ireland Assembly. This action was taken by the British government In order to protect the Good Friday Agreement, after Unionists accused the Republicans of not being completely committed to peaceful politics.

Controversy

The devolution of power to Scotland and Wales has been seen as one of the most significant developments of the British constitution for many years. It has aroused great controversy.

Break up of the UK

Some people feel that giving power to the Scottish Parliament and Welsh Assembly destroys the unity of the UK and leads to greater division between the different nations.

Others believe that the overall authority of the UK Parliament remains, since it can at any time repeal the two Acts that devolved power to Scotland and Wales.

Disagreement

Some people are concerned that a disagreement between the Scottish and UK Parliaments may lead to a constitutional crisis about which has the greater authority. There are safeguards to overcome this difficulty included in the *Scotland Act*, but there are concerns about whether these would be enough.

The 'West Lothian question'

In the 1970s, Tam Dalyell, then MP for West Lothian in Scotland, warned of the consequences of introducing a separate Scottish Parliament. One result, he said, would be that a Scottish MP in Westminster could vote on issues like health and education affecting England, but not when they applied to Scotland, as these matters would be devolved to a Scottish Parliament.

As Scotland now has its own Parliament, some believe that Scottish MPs in the UK Parliament should have less power, and should not be able to vote at Westminster about issues that do not affect Scotland. Others argue that Westminster remains the UK Parliament and that all MPs have the right to take part in any of its business.

Hospital vote

In July 2003, the House of Commons voted on a controversial government proposal to change the way some hospitals were run. The government won the vote by a majority of only 35. Their opponents argued that the support of Scottish MPs was crucial to this victory – but the proposal will not apply to any hospitals in Scotland.

Beyond central government

Regional government

For many years, concerns have been expressed that too much power in Britain is centralised in London. In order to give people in the regions of England more control over their affairs, the government announced plans in 2002 to hold a series of referendums on whether people wanted a new level of regional government. These assemblies, it was proposed, would make decisions on local issues concerned with transport, housing and the environment.

The first referendum was held in the North East in 2004 and the proposal was rejected. Shortly afterwards, the planned referendums in Yorkshire and Humber and the North West were postponed.

Outside Scotland, Wales and Northern Ireland, London is the only region of the UK to have a form of elected regional government.

Governing London

In 2000, the government established the Greater London Authority (GLA) to provide regional government for the whole of the London area. The authority has responsibility for London's transport system, economic development, the Metropolitan Police and London's fire service. The GLA is made up of a Mayor and an Assembly, each elected for a four-year term.

The Mayor of London

The office of the Mayor of London was created by the *Greater London Authority Act* in 1999. One reason for doing this was to bring London into line with other major cities of the world, such as Paris and New York.

Duties

The Mayor of London has to set out the policy and budget for the GLA. Other organisations, such as 'Transport for London' then put this into practice. The 'London Plan' sets out the Mayor's policy for planning and use of land that all parts of London must follow. The Mayor also has the task of representing the interests of London, both in the UK and abroad. The Mayor of London was part of the team that bid for the Olympic Games to be held in London in 2012.

Congestion charge

As part of his transport policy Ken Livingston, Mayor of London, wished to encourage more people to use public transport and to help traffic move more quickly in London. In February 2003, Transport for London introduced a congestion charge for drivers entering the central area of the capital. The initial effect of this was to reduce traffic by about 20 per cent.

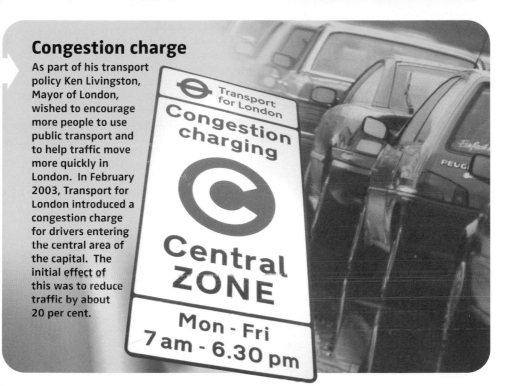

The London Assembly

The 25 members of the Assembly have to approve the Mayor's budget each year and examine the Mayor's decisions. The Mayor must consult the Assembly and make sure that the Assembly is kept informed of all major decisions. He or she must attend at least ten meetings of the Assembly each year and answer questions in person.

While in office, Assembly members are required to take decisions as far as possible in full public view. For example, meetings of the Assembly are public and the records of meetings and papers submitted to the Assembly and its reports must be made available to the public.

The Mayor and Assembly attend a twice yearly People's Question Time at which the public can put questions to them. In addition, the ten meetings a year where the Assembly question the Mayor are open to the public. For further details, see **www.london.gov.uk**.

Other regions

The government has created nine Regional Development Agencies in England to promote economic development. Each of these has a non-elected assembly made up of representatives from local authorities, business and industry within the region. Their role is to co-ordinate transport, planning, economic development, and bids for European funding.

Beyond central government

Local government

Towns, cities and rural areas in the UK are administered by a system of local government or councils, often known as local authorities. They are responsible for delivering a range of community services including education, social services, public transport, housing, libraries and environmental health.

Local authorities work within the powers laid down under various Acts of Parliament. Their functions are far-reaching. Some are mandatory, which means that the authority must do what is required by law. Others are discretionary, allowing an authority to provide a service if it wishes.

Background

The first attempts to organise local government in Britain were not made until the nineteenth century when Britain became an industrialised and urban society. Local government had changed very little since the 1600s and was still carried out by a range of different unelected officials and organisations.

The rapid growth of towns brought problems of housing and public health that the old system could not deal with. Some city councils, principally Birmingham, Leeds and Manchester, took the initiative in tackling these problems, but by the end of the century there was an urgent need for a system of local government that could bring improvements for all local areas.

Elected councils

In 1888, Parliament began to set up a structure of elected county, district and borough councils to cover the whole of England and Wales. By the 1930s local government was responsible for supplying housing, health and education, and also the management of water, gas and electricity supplies.

Developments

The role of local councils has changed considerably over the last 60 years. They now provide far fewer services than in the past. For example, they no longer manage electricity, water and gas supplies. Today it is the role of local government to ensure that these services are available to local residents.

The structure of local councils has also been changed since they were set up in the nineteenth century. Reorganisation has taken

Hunting ban refused

Somerset County Council wanted to ban deer hunting over land that it had recently bought for use by its residents. The Court of Appeal, however, said that it could not do this, since it had not been given the authority by Parliament to make a decision of this kind. It was not lawful, the Court said, for the council to take this action over a "sensitive national issue" until it had been resolved by Parliament.

place several times, particularly since the 1970s, and today, the pattern of local government varies from one part of the country to another.

Central control

Local government in Britain is largely controlled by central government. The only powers that local authorities have are those handed down by the UK Parliament. Their main responsibilities and duties are set out by central government, allowing councils to decide the best way to meet local needs and provide services within their area.

Sometimes local authorities may try to resist the power of central government. However they are rarely successful, since the supreme power of Parliament is a key principle of the UK constitution.

Finance

Most of the money local government receives each year is given to councils by central government. About 25 per cent comes from funds the council collects from its area through council tax.

During the 1980s the government was concerned by what was thought to be a high level of spending by councils. It introduced a number of measures to 'cap' or limit, spending. Strict government controls remain in force today. Councils are prevented from charging too high a level of council tax and have little freedom in how they allocate their funds.

Tax limits

In 2005, Hambleton District Council in North Yorkshire had to scrap plans for community improvements costing £300,000 after the government blocked a proposed increase of 17 per cent in the local council tax. The Council was intending to use the money to install CCTV cameras, employ street wardens and upgrade recycling facilities. Hambleton was one of eight councils in the UK to be affected by the capping order, which the government said was necessary to stop excessive increases in council tax.

Beyond central government

Council elections

Local councils are elected for a four-year term of office. Local councillors represent an area known as a 'ward'. The voting system is generally the same as that used in general elections, where the candidate with a simple majority of votes is elected, see page 128. Some wards return more than one councillor and in these areas the voting system differs slightly.

Councillors

A candidate for election to a local council must be able to show a close connection with the area. He or she must be on the local register of electors, or have lived or worked in the local authority area for at least a year before being nominated for election. There are restrictions on standing for council for those who are bankrupt, or have recent criminal convictions.

Most councillors are not paid for council work, but they can claim expenses and allowances.

Many have full-time jobs. They must attend at least one council meeting every six months.

Duties

There is no set job description for local councillors, but there are certain roles that they are expected to carry out:

- **representing constituents – for example, dealing with problems of schooling, housing or planning**
- **taking part in council and committee meetings**
- **monitoring the work of the council leaders and officers.**

Corruption

All councils must follow a code of conduct, and councillors must declare if they have any financial interest in council business. Councillors are expected to show high standards of conduct, especially in financial matters.

Bribery

Architect John Poulson, was found guilty of corruption at Leeds Crown Court and sentenced to five years in prison. It was alleged that he had spent more than £500,000 on suits, holidays and flowers to bribe councillors and other officials into awarding building contracts to his company. After he was jailed, John Poulson confessed to another nine cases of corruption and conspiracy and received a further two-year prison sentence.

Management

Until recently, local councils were organised around a system of committees. Each one covered a particular area, such as education, housing or planning, and then reported back to the full council. But since the *Local Government Act 2000* came into force, this has changed considerably.

Day-to-day decisions about the running of the council are now made by a small group of senior councillors, known as a cabinet, with one councillor acting as leader. It is the job of the full council to approve general policy and to monitor the work of the leader and cabinet.

The new mayors

Another significant change introduced by the *Local Government Act 2000* has been the opportunity for residents of towns and cities with a population of more than 85,000 to decide by a referendum whether they wish to have an elected mayor.

Those in favour of the idea see it as a way of getting more people interested in local politics and giving them a say in how things are run. Supporters also argue that putting one person in charge makes it harder for excuses to be given when things go wrong and promises are not kept.

By 2006, referendums had been held in 32 areas of England and Wales on whether to have an elected mayor, and the people of twelve towns and cities had voted in favour of this.

The office of mayor

Known as the Lord Mayor in cities and as a provost or Lord Provost in Scotland, the office of mayor is an ancient part of local government. There are records of mayors in some towns and cities that go back nearly 1,000 years. Originally mayors had wide powers in running the affairs of the town or city, but many of these were lost in the nineteenth century as local government became more democratic.

Today the work of the mayor or provost in most places is largely ceremonial, though he or she still presides over meetings of the council and has a duty to make sure that they are conducted in a proper manner.

Consultation

When drawing up plans for the community, councils are required to consult and work closely with local organisations, like businesses, voluntary associations and residents' groups.

Britain & the wider world

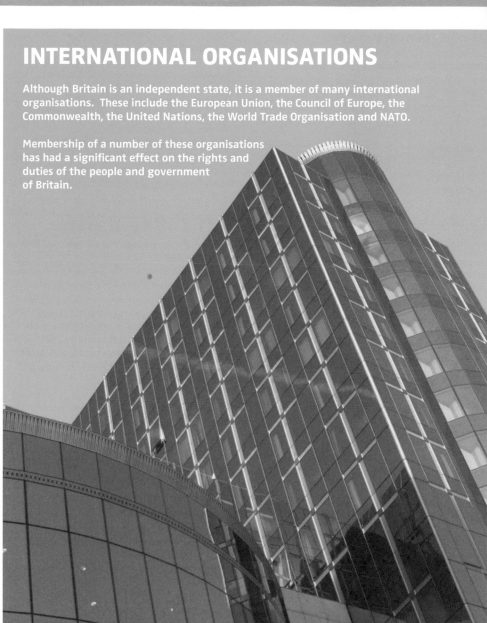

INTERNATIONAL ORGANISATIONS

Although Britain is an independent state, it is a member of many international organisations. These include the European Union, the Council of Europe, the Commonwealth, the United Nations, the World Trade Organisation and NATO.

Membership of a number of these organisations has had a significant effect on the rights and duties of the people and government of Britain.

The European Union

About 50 million people died in the Second World War. When it ended in 1945, governments throughout Europe wanted to do something that would help guarantee peace and rebuild their battered nations. They decided to co-operate in a number of ways.

In 1951, six countries (Belgium, France, Italy, Luxembourg, the Netherlands and West Germany) agreed to place all their coal and steel production under the control of a single European authority, known as the European Coal and Steel Community. This, it was hoped, would make war both unthinkable and practically impossible.

In 1957, the same states signed the Treaty of Rome, aiming to create a single market (one large trading area) where trade barriers would be removed and people, goods and services could move freely around member states. This became known as the European Economic Community (EEC) or Common Market. During the 1970s, more states – including Britain – joined the EEC.

Today there are 25 member states and the organisation is known as the European Union. Making it easier for members to trade with one another is still one of its main aims, but co-operation has been extended to many other areas including agriculture, the environment, international crime, immigration and foreign policy.

Structure

The European Union is the term given to the whole area of co-operation and integration between member states.

One way in which the EU is often represented is as the roof of a building, supported by three pillars – each representing different areas of co-operation.

The first pillar illustrates all the ways in which member states act as a single body, taking decisions together, often by majority vote. These include decisions about trade, agriculture and fishing, the environment, immigration and the rights of people to move from one state to another.

The second pillar covers areas of common foreign and security policy; and the third deals with police and judicial co-operation in criminal matters. Decisions about issues in both of these pillars are taken on what is known as an inter-governmental basis. This means that member states must all agree on decisions that are reached, allowing states to retain their sovereignty or independence.

Britain & the wider world

Institutions

The European Union (EU) is governed by a number of institutions, which make laws, set policies and make sure that member states follow the agreements that they have signed up to.

Council of the European Union

The Council (often referred to as the Council of Ministers) is the main decision-making body of the EU, with the power to make EU laws and to decide how EU money will be spent.

It is made up of ministers from each member state and is the only EU institution representing member states' national governments. Ministers attend according to the issues being discussed. For example, if the discussion is about farming, the UK will be represented by the Secretary of State for Environment, Food and Rural Affairs.

Generally speaking, Council decisions are taken by a system of majority voting. There are some issues on which ministers are required to be unanimous, but these are dwindling. They include common foreign and security policy, police, justice and criminal affairs (pillars two and three, see page 105), new treaties, the enlargement of the EU, and certain questions about the EU budget.

Two or three times a year the Council holds a summit meeting of all heads of state, also known as the European Council. Members of this meeting cannot make laws, but they do set the political agenda for the EU.

The European Parliament

The European Parliament is responsible for debating and passing laws, and is the only directly elected body of the EU.

It is made up of 732 MEPs (Members of the European Parliament) elected from the 25 member states. Seats in the European Parliament are shared out amongst member states on the basis of the country's population. There are 78 UK MEPs.

Elections Elections for MEPs are held every five years. Voting in European Parliamentary elections is open to any EU citizen, providing they are on the list of electors.

Contact and petition Debates in the European Parliament buildings in Brussels and Strasbourg are open to the public, and MEPs can be reached by e-mail or post or phone at their constituency office.

Residents of the EU can petition the European Parliament on any issue that comes under the EU remit and directly affects them. The petition may be a complaint or a request for a particular policy to be adopted. The petition can be by post or e-mail and must include the sender's name, address, and nationality.

The European Commission

The European Commission is a powerful organisation within the EU. It has several functions.

Firstly it is the Commission's job to make sure that member states keep to the agreements and treaties they have made. Secondly, it is responsible for proposing new EU laws, which then need to be approved by the European Parliament and Council of Ministers. Thirdly, the Commission puts into place decisions made by the European Parliament and the Council.

There are 25 Commissioners, at the moment, one for each member state. Each Commissioner is responsible for a different area of work.

The European Court of Justice

The European Court of Justice is based in Luxembourg and is responsible for ensuring that member states correctly follow and apply EU law.

The Court is made up of senior judges from each member state, who hold office for six years. It is the most senior court in Europe and overrules all national courts. Member states must follow its decisions.

Net fine

In 2005, the European Court of Justice fined France 20m euros (£14m) for breaking EU fishing laws designed to protect fish stocks. The Court also ordered France to pay a further 57.8m euros every six months until it fully complies with the law.

The Court criticised France for allowing undersized fish to be offered for sale and for not taking strong enough action against those who broke the law.

Britain & the wider world

Britain and the EU

Background

In 1950, Britain was invited to join discussions with the six states in forming the European Coal and Steel Community. The government declined, believing that it would be better to concentrate on its relations with the Commonwealth, rather than Europe. It was also worried that the kind of co-operation being planned would mean a loss of sovereignty for Britain, and would place the country under the authority of a higher body able to tell it what it could and could not do.

By the late 1950s, however, most of Britain's trade was with Europe and not the Commonwealth, and in 1961, Britain applied for membership of what, by this time, was known as the European Economic Community. This and a further application were rejected twice by France. Britain was eventually admitted to the EEC in 1972, and joined on 1st January 1973.

Citizens' rights

All British citizens are also citizens of the European Union. This provides people with additional rights.

Travel Citizens of EU member states have the right to travel to any EU country, as long as they have a valid passport or identity card. This right may be restricted only for reasons of public order, public security or public health.

Residence EU citizens have the right to live anywhere in the EU. Those who choose to live in another member state, must have a job, or be able to show that they have enough resources to support themselves. It is not possible to claim welfare benefits in another member state. EU citizens can also study in other EU member states.

Referendum

In 1975, British Labour Prime Minister Harold Wilson gave voters the chance to decide whether or not Britain should stay in the European Common Market. It was the first and only UK national referendum.

Three years earlier Britain had joined the Common Market, under the leadership of Conservative Prime Minister Edward Heath – but membership remained controversial. The Labour government, which came to power in 1974, re-negotiated the terms of entry and called a referendum for their approval, resulting in a majority of two-to-one for staying in.

Voting EU citizens living in another member state have the right to vote in local and European elections, if they are on the electoral register. They are not able, however, to vote in national elections.

Work EU citizens have the right to work anywhere in the EU, and should be offered employment under the same conditions as citizens of that state.

European and British law
European Union law is superior to national law and national constitutions. This means that member states must comply with European law and parliaments cannot make laws that undermine this.

If a country fails to implement EU laws, it can be taken to the European Court of Justice, see page 107.

The European Union's law-making powers, however, do not cover all areas of life. They are generally confined to those matters included in pillar one (page 105), that is employment, trade, industry, agriculture, fishing, immigration and rights of travel. The areas covered in pillars two and three (page 105) tend to be more sensitive and are areas where national governments want to be able to retain more control over decision-making.

New rights

In 2001, European Union employment and social affairs ministers agreed a new law requiring all companies operating in the EU to inform employees about any decision affecting their jobs – especially if it might lead to redundancies. The governments of Britain and Ireland, who both opposed the law, were given seven years to put it into practice.

Britain & the wider world

 ## The Council of Europe

The Council of Europe was established in 1949, four years after the end of the Second World War. It is located in Strasbourg, in north east France, and was set up to protect and promote human rights and democracy. Although the names sound similar, it is not part of the European Union, and has no connection with the Council of Ministers or European Council, see page 106.

The Council of Europe has exerted considerable influence in Europe, particularly through the European Convention on Human Rights. Today the Council has 46 member states. Each one has agreed to follow the Convention (known as ratification), and many, including Britain, have incorporated its principles into their own laws.

European Convention on Human Rights

This is an international agreement, signed and drawn up in 1950, setting out the basic human rights and freedoms that all governments should provide for everyone in their country. The main rights under the Convention include:

- **the right to life**
- **the right to liberty**
- **the right to a fair trial**
- **respect for private and family life, home and correspondence**
- **freedom of thought, conscience and religion**
- **freedom of speech**
- **freedom of peaceful assembly**
- **the right to marry and start a family**
- **prohibition of torture and slavery.**

Convention rights must not be unfairly restricted – unless it can be justified for reasons of public safety, the prevention of crime, the rights of others or national security.

Making the Convention part of UK law

The *Human Rights Act 1998* incorporates nearly all the rights contained in the Convention into UK law. Under this Act, all our laws must as far as possible follow the rights listed in the Convention and all public bodies must carry out their work in a way that respects these human rights. If they don't, then the law or the public body can be challenged in a UK court.

European Court of Human Rights

This Court was established in 1959 and is made up of a Judge from each member state. It is responsible for ensuring that member states keep to their obligations set out in the Convention.

Anyone may take a case to the Court, but they must first have exhausted all legal possibilities at home. Cases are brought against the state, not private bodies or individuals.

Countries must follow the decision of the Court, although the Court cannot directly enforce this.

Barred from voting

In October 2005, the European Court of Human Rights ruled that Britain's ban on the right of a prisoner to vote was in breach of the European Convention on Human Rights.

The case was taken to Strasbourg by John Hirst, who had been sentenced to life imprisonment for manslaughter. He thought that the ban was an unjust additional punishment and incompatible with the *Human Rights Act*. His case was first heard at the High Court in London, which ruled that the ban on prisoners voting was not unlawful. The European Court of Human Right's verdict overrules this decision and requires the British government to change the existing law to give some, if not all, prisoners the right to vote.

The Commonwealth

From the sixteenth century onwards, Britain began to take control of a number of overseas territories, building up what was to become one of the largest empires in history. At its height, the British Empire included about a quarter of the world's population.

However, the American Declaration of Independence in 1776 was an early sign of rebellion against British control – and over the next 200 years almost all the states within the Empire became independent.

By the early twentieth century, states such as Canada, Australia, New Zealand and South Africa were all free to decide their own government, and it was around this time that the idea of 'commonwealth' began to replace 'empire'. Newly independent countries started to be seen as part of an association of states – equal and not inferior to Britain, as they had been in the past.

The Commonwealth today is made up of 53 member states – all of whom (except Namibia and Mozambique) were part of the former British Empire. It has no constitution or charter, and does not have any legal power. However, all member countries must commit themselves to principles of human rights, equality, and democracy. As a voluntary association of nations from all parts of the world, the Commonwealth has a powerful voice in international debate.

Britain & the wider world

The Queen as Head of State

Most Commonwealth countries are now completely independent of Britain. More than 30 Commonwealth nations, such as India and Pakistan, are republics with their own head of state. Five have national monarchies of their own, and 16, such as Australia and Canada, have Queen Elizabeth II as Head of State.

In those countries where the Queen has been kept as Head of State, she is represented by a Governor General, appointed by the Queen on advice from the government of the country concerned. The Governor General's position is similar, in for example Canada, to the monarch's position in the UK.

As the head of the Commonwealth, the Queen has no power to rule. She is seen as the symbolic head of a free association of states.

Legal ties

Almost all Commonwealth states today are self-governing – developing their own rules and laws independently from Britain.

Some of their laws and legal systems, however, do still contain signs of past links with Britain. One of the most unusual, in this respect, is for the Privy Council to act as a final court of appeal in important civil cases and in criminal cases where the offender has been sentenced to death. This right has been retained in many Caribbean countries and Mauritius.

Final Decision

In 2003, the government of Belize decided to approve the construction of a large dam in one of the most undisturbed areas of wilderness in Central America. Environmentalists argued that the plan would have a devastating impact on wildlife. The Belize government disagreed, saying that it would provide an important source of electricity. In 2004, five senior UK judges were asked to decide on this issue. By three votes to two, they allowed the building of the dam to go ahead, on the grounds that it would not pose the threat to animals and wildlife that was feared.

The Australian referendum

In 1999, twelve million Australians took part in a compulsory referendum to decide whether to keep the Queen as head of state or to become a republic and replace her with a president.

By a vote of 55 to 45 per cent, they rejected the idea of breaking ties with Britain, and Queen Elizabeth II continues as Queen of Australia. Some commentators, however, believe that one reason for the republicans' defeat was because the referendum proposed that the president would be chosen by the Australian Parliament – and not by the people.

The United Nations

The United Nations was established in 1945, just after the end of the Second World War, with the main aim of keeping world peace. Britain was of the 51 founding members. Today 191 countries belong to the UN – almost every nation in the world.

All member states must sign the UN Charter. This is an international treaty under which members agree to respect human rights, to keep the peace between nations and to co-operate together over international problems.

The United Nations doesn't make laws, but does try to provide ways of getting nations to work together to deal with international difficulties.

The General Assembly

The General Assembly is the main parliament of the UN, and is based in New York. All member states have a seat in the Assembly, and each has one vote.

The main function of the General Assembly is to discuss any matter that is covered by the UN Charter. This covers a wide range of topics.

Agenda

At its meeting in September 2005, subjects discussed by the General Assembly included: the situation in the Middle East, the Falkland Islands, human rights in Haiti, the establishment of nuclear-weapon-free zones, emergency assistance for people in Afghanistan, reducing world poverty and climate change.

The Assembly cannot force a country to act in a particular way, but its recommendations are an important indication of world opinion. They are a powerful way of telling a member state what the rest of the world thinks that it should or should not be doing.

Britain & the wider world

The Security Council

One of the most powerful organisations in the UN is the Security Council, made up of representatives from 15 member states. There are five permanent members – China, France, Russia, the United Kingdom and the United States. The remaining ten places are taken by other UN countries on a rotating basis. Membership lasts for two years. There is general agreement that the number of permanent members should be increased to include representatives from Asia, Africa and South America, but existing Security Council members cannot agree on how this should be done.

An important function of the Security Council is to deal with disagreements that threaten peace between member states. In a dispute, the Council will try to find ways of getting both sides to agree. However, if this fails and fighting breaks out, it may send in a peace-keeping force to try to separate the opposing forces and help restore peace. If the conflict continues, the Security Council can order UN member states to impose economic sanctions (such as a ban on trade) and in some circumstances may authorise military action.

Restoring peace

The state of East Timor, Timor-Leste, as it is now known, is part of the Island of Timor, located about 400 miles north of Australia.

In the sixteenth century the island was settled by the Portuguese, who colonised and ruled East Timor for nearly 400 years.

In 1974, a new government in Portugal decided to grant independence to all the country's overseas territories, and in November 1975, East Timor declared itself independent. Nine days later, it was invaded by neighbouring Indonesia. Over the next 25 years, in the occupation that followed, thousands of people in East Timor were killed.

In 1998, the president of Indonesia resigned, and shortly afterwards the people of East Timor were offered independence from Indonesia. Not everyone in the Indonesian armed forces

accepted this, and serious fighting again broke out as groups tried to prevent the country moving out of Indonesian control. The UN Security Council acted quickly, and in September 1999, ordered a peace-keeping force to East Timor, led by Australia. It stayed there until 2005.

Human rights

The protection of human rights was one of the main reasons for the creation of the United Nations. There are two particularly important human rights documents produced by the UN: the Universal Declaration of Human Rights and the UN Convention on the Rights of the Child. Neither has the force of law, but both give a clear indication of the standards that countries are expected to achieve.

Care of children in the UK

In 2002, a report by the UN Committee on the Rights of the Child strongly criticised the British government over the treatment of children in the UK. Amongst the Committee's concerns were the numbers of children excluded from school, the numbers held in custody and conditions in young offenders' institutions. The report also recommended a change in the law to prevent parents from being able to hit their children.

Since 2002, the UK government has amended the law on corporal punishment, but the government continues to reject an outright ban on smacking.

Breaches of human rights

The UN Human Rights Commissioner investigates cases where governments are suspected of abusing people's human rights. If there is evidence that a serious breach of human rights has taken place, an attempt will be made to put the suspect on trial at the International Criminal Tribunal at The Hague in Holland.

Treaties

Quite often, two or more countries will sign a treaty – agreeing some form of co-operation. UK governments sign treaties on all kinds of issues. Some of these are through their membership of the United Nations. One of the best-known examples is the Kyoto Protocol – a global agreement to reduce the emission of greenhouse gases linked to global warming and climate change. The treaty was drawn up in 1997 and signed by most (but not all) industrial nations.

Parliament in Britain is not directly involved in making agreements of this kind. It is something that the government does alone. However, under a voluntary government agreement made in 1924, the government will inform Parliament of all new treaties, and then wait 21 days before signing. This is designed to allow the treaty to be discussed in Parliament, and for a formal debate to take place, if required.

Britain & the wider world

▶ The World Trade Organisation

The World Trade Organisation (WTO) was established in 1995 and is based in Geneva in Switzerland. It is an international body that creates and enforces rules of trade. These rules are designed to help countries trade with one another in a fair and open way and to lower the tariffs, or taxes, that countries often impose on imported goods. One hundred and forty-nine countries belong to the WTO.

Rules of trade

Members of the WTO have together created a large number of trade agreements. Before each agreement is finalised it is approved (or ratified) by the Parliament of each member state. The agreement then becomes legally binding, and must be followed by all members.

Settling disputes

When an agreement is broken or a dispute arises between two countries, the WTO will investigate the case and produce a ruling, along with a timetable of how and when the ruling should be put into practice. The decision of the WTO is absolute and must be followed by all sides.

A bitter taste

In 2002, Australia, Brazil and Thailand, three of the world's biggest sugar cane exporters, lodged a complaint with the World Trade Organisation over the subsidies that the European Union was paying its sugar beet farmers.

The governments of the three nations claimed that the money paid by the EU to its farmers gave the farmers an unfair advantage by allowing them to sell sugar at a lower price than that at which it could be produced. It also made it much harder, they argued, for farmers in countries like their own not offering subsidies, to sell their sugar overseas.

In 2004 the WTO ruled that the subsidies the EU paid to its sugar beet farmers broke WTO rules. The EU agreed to cut the subsidy it paid to its farmers, by the middle of 2006, by 36 per cent.

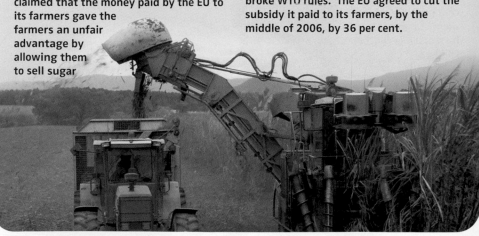

DEMOCRACY AND JUSTICE

3

Parliament	page **118**
Law, courts & judges	page **134**

Parliament

THE WESTMINSTER PARLIAMENT

The UK Parliament at Westminster is very old. A royal palace, going back to the twelfth century, originally stood on the present site, and today the Parliament is still known as the Palace of Westminster. Work on the present building began in 1840, after fire destroyed much of the old palace. It was completed in 1860.

Through history, Parliament has evolved from a council that advised the monarch to the present day legislature. It is made up of three parts – the House of Commons, the House of Lords and the Monarch.

Parliament is the supreme law-making body in the United Kingdom, and may pass a law on any matter it wishes. It does not have to follow decisions made by an earlier Parliament, nor can it try to restrict the power of future Parliaments. However, in practice there are limitations in what it can do as a result of Britain's membership of the European Union and other international agreements that the UK has entered into.

The role of Parliament

Parliament has four main functions, to:

- **examine and vote on proposals for new laws**
- **examine and check government policy**
- **debate the major issues of the day**
- **authorise the government's plans for raising and spending money.**

Parliament is not the same as government, although members of the government are also Members of Parliament. It is Parliament's job to scrutinise the actions and work of government.

Further details about the work and functioning of Parliament can be found at:
www.parliament.uk or
www.explore.parliament.uk.

Voting on new laws

A proposal for a new law is known as a Bill. For a Bill to become law it must go through several stages of discussion and debate in both the House of Commons and the House of Lords. When these have been completed a Bill receives the royal assent (see page 88) and becomes law. It is then known as a statute or Act of Parliament.

Under the *Parliament Acts 1911* and *1949* the House of Lords may not block a Bill that has been approved by the House of Commons. Since 1949 the House of Lords has had power only to delay the passage of a Bill by a year.

Parliament can also agree to a number of Bills introduced by backbench MPs, see page 124. These are called private member's Bills and generally deal with questions of interest to minority groups or those which may be too

controversial for a government to take the lead. The current law on abortion originated as a private member's Bill.

Divisions

Members of the House of Commons and House of Lords do not vote by mechanical or electronic means. They vote by division.

In the Commons, those voting 'Aye' (yes) to a proposition walk through the Division Lobby, or corridor, to the right of the Speaker and those voting 'No' through the lobby to the left.

The Speaker, who presides over debates, calls for a vote by announcing, "Clear the Lobbies". Division bells ring throughout the building and the police walk through the public rooms of the House shouting "division". MPs have eight minutes to get to the Division Lobby before the doors are closed.

Parliament

A shorter route

Each year Parliament passes about 40 new Acts of Parliament, known as primary legislation.

These laws, however, cannot always cover every rule or regulation surrounding the subject that they deal with. To prevent Bills from becoming too long and to avoid the need for an Act every time something needs to be updated, Acts of Parliament may include sections that give the government powers to make updates or amendments at a later stage. These are called statutory instruments and about 3,500 are issued each year.

Laws of this kind are known as secondary legislation, and their use is sometimes controversial. This is because secondary legislation is not checked and examined by Parliament as thoroughly as primary legislation, and the number of regulations of this type can make it difficult for people to discover what the law says.

Scrutinising the government

In the past, Parliament had the job of trying to make sure that the king or queen did not exceed their power. Today it has the same critical role in scrutinising the government, to make sure that it governs in the best interests of the people.

Both Houses of Parliament carry out this function in a number of ways.

Questioning ministers

Each Wednesday between 12–12.30pm, when Parliament is in session, the Prime Minister must attend the House of Commons to answer questions from the Leader of the Opposition (see page 124) and other MPs. Other senior ministers must answer questions in Parliament at least once a month about the work of their department.

MPs and members of the House of Lords also put forward written questions to find out more about government policy and actions. There were almost 30,000 written questions to ministers during the 2004–2005 session of Parliament. Departments must respond to these questions within set time limits.

Debates

As well as debates about proposed new laws, there are also opportunities for debating government action. The Opposition parties in the House of Commons have the right to choose the subject for debate on 20 days each session. Also, at the end of normal business on most days there are 'adjournment debates' when MPs can raise issues and grievances about government action. Debates also take place away from the main Chamber. These are known as Westminster Hall debates.

ality Act 2006

CHAPTER 3

Consolidated Fund A...

European Union (Accessions) Act 2006

acial and Religious Hatred Act 2006

CHAPTER 1

CONTENTS

ance (No. 2)

Select Committees

An important way for Parliament to scrutinise the work of the government is through Select Committees. These are composed of a small number of back bench MPs or members of the House of Lords.

Select Committees have wide powers to call ministers and civil servants to appear before them and answer detailed questions about the work of government. Each Committee presents a written report of its findings to Parliament.

Debating major issues

Both Houses of Parliament may choose to debate important issues. Sometimes the Speaker will suspend the normal business of the Commons to allow for an emergency debate on a particularly important and urgent matter.

In the House of Lords, debates on topical issues are held each Thursday afternoon. These cover a wide range of subjects from co-operation between Christianity and Islam to the decline of the red squirrel.

Finance

Constitutional arrangements for controlling the finance needed to run the country have been in place since the seventeenth century. Since that time it has been established that the government must have the approval of Parliament, and the House of Commons in particular, to levy taxes and to spend public money. However Parliament cannot put forward its own proposals for expenditure. It may only respond to government proposals.

Since the *Parliament Act 1911* only the House of Commons, rather than Parliament as a whole, has had the power to authorise government use of finance.

The 'People's Budget'

In 1909 a major crisis arose over Parliament's control of finance. The Liberal government presented a Budget (its annual estimate of revenue and expenditure) that would enable it to introduce a programme of radical social reforms, including the first old age pensions. The House of Lords, mostly composed at that time of Conservative peers, refused to accept the Budget. This broke a long-standing convention that gave the House of Commons the sole power to raise taxes.

A year later in two general elections, the government secured the support of the people for its pension proposal, and for reform of the House of Lords.

As a result, the *Parliament Act* was passed in 1911. It stated, amongst other changes, that the House of Lords had no power over measures concerning taxation or public money.

Parliament

Parliament and the public

There are a number of ways in which the public can find out about what is happening in Parliament.

Hansard

The official report of the proceedings of Parliament is known as Hansard, named after Thomas Hansard who published a daily record of the Commons in the nineteenth century.

Hansard is still published each day when Parliament is sitting and records everything that is said and done in both the House of Commons and House of Lords, for which separate reports are issued. Hansard is also available from the UK Parliament website, **www.parliament.uk**.

Public galleries

There are galleries in both Houses of Parliament from which members of the public can watch

and listen to debates. Most sittings of Select Committees (see page 121) are also open to the public. However, access to both the galleries and committees is limited. Details of visits to Parliament are available from **www.parliament.uk**.

Broadcasts

Live coverage for Parliament, including most Select Committees is available via Parliament's Internet service at **www.parliamentlive.tv**. BBC Parliament broadcasts live unedited coverage of the House of Commons on cable, satellite and Freeview. BBC Radio has a daily programme of excerpts from proceedings in Parliament.

The press

The press are entitled to report on proceedings in Parliament and each House of Parliament has a gallery for the use of journalists.

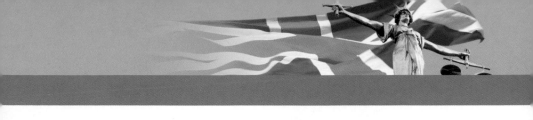

The House of Commons

Convention

Tradition and convention are very important in the procedures of the House of Commons. It has its own rules, known as Standing Orders, which govern the ways in which the House conducts its business and how MPs behave in debates.

Tradition

It is traditional that, when speaking in the House of Commons and House of Lords, members do not refer to the other House by name. Instead they describe it as 'Another Place'

During a debate in the House of Commons, MPs refer to each other only by the name of their constituencies or by their official position, not their actual names. The only time names are used is when the Speaker calls MPs to speak or disciplines them.

The party system

Modern political parties in Britain began to develop in the nineteenth century as more and more people (always men) were given the vote. Groups of like-minded MPs began to organise themselves on a national basis in the hope of attracting more votes and thereby remaining in power.

The political party with the most MPs in the House of Commons is the party of government, led by the Prime Minister.

The Speaker

The Speaker is an MP who has been elected by the other MPs to chair the debates in the House of Commons. It is his or her responsibility to make sure that the rules laid down by the House for carrying out its business are observed. It is the Speaker who calls MPs to speak, and maintains order in the House. The Speaker must be impartial in all matters and once elected takes no part in party politics.

In 1642, during the struggle between King and Parliament, King Charles I brought armed followers into the House of Commons seeking to arrest five parliamentary leaders. The King asked where they were. The Speaker replied that he had "neither eyes to see nor tongue to speak" except as the House of Commons commanded him. This is still the position of the Speaker today.

Parliament

Whips

Whips are MPs who are appointed by each party to keep party discipline. Their main role is to encourage members of their party to vote in the way that their party would like. They are believed to take their name from 'whippers-in' – the men who controlled packs of hunting hounds.

The party of government

The governing party always sits on the benches to the right of the Speaker. The Prime Minister and members of the government sit on the front bench. The Leader of the House of Commons is the member of the government who is responsible for organising business in the Commons.

In order to remain in power, the Prime Minister and his or her government must be able to get support for their main policies from the House of Commons. This includes getting their proposed new laws (Bills) approved, securing agreement for taxation and public expenditure and defeating the Opposition in debates on motions criticising the government.

The Opposition

The Opposition are the political parties other than the largest or government party. They are called the Opposition because they sit on the benches opposite the government in the House of Commons Chamber. The largest of the Opposition parties is known as Her Majesty's Loyal Opposition to signify their loyalty to the Crown, as distinct from the policies of her ministers.

The Opposition questions the government about its actions and policies to check that the country is being properly managed. It opposes new laws with which it disagrees and promotes its own policies as an alternative.

Leader of the Opposition

The leader of the second largest party in the House of Commons has the title Leader of Her Majesty's Loyal Opposition. He or she is entitled to a salary for this post and sits on the Opposition Front Bench.

The Opposition Party appoints an MP to 'shadow' each member of the Cabinet. This group is known as the Shadow Cabinet and sits on the front benches to the left of the Speaker.

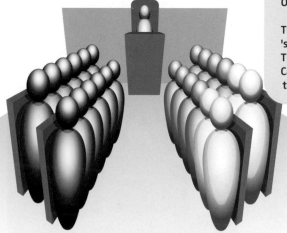

Backbenchers

An MP who holds no official position in government, or in his or her party, sits on the back benches of the Chamber and is known as a back bench MP or backbencher.

Members of Parliament

An MP has a range of responsibilities to carry out. Some of these are linked to his or her constituents, some to their political party, and some to their position as a member of the House of Commons.

Constituents

An MP represents everybody who lives in the constituency that she or he represents in Parliament. This includes those who did not vote for him or her. A large part of an MP's work is to do with constituency concerns and problems.

Although MPs represent the views of their constituents in Parliament, they are not required to follow these when they vote. Sometimes MPs feel obliged to follow their own beliefs. To find out how your MP voted in debates and how often they attend Parliament see **www.theyworkforyou.com** and **www.publicwhip.org.uk**.

Personal belief

In using their best judgment in their role as MP, Members of Parliament may not always reflect the views of their constituents; and those who don't, occasionally run the risk of losing their seat. Between 1997 and 2001, Jackie Ballard was Liberal-Democrat MP for Taunton in Somerset. During this time, she was very critical of the deer hunting that took place in her constituency. She lost her seat in the 2001 election, and some argued that an important reason for this was her opposition to hunting.

Party demands

MPs are expected to support their party in debates and votes in the House of Commons. MPs who are disloyal to their party run the risk of not being promoted and may even be forced to resign from the party.

Resignation

Constitutionally, MPs may not simply resign from their seat. Instead they must apply for one of two ancient Crown offices. These are the Crown Steward and Bailiff of the Chiltern Hundreds, and the Manor of Northstead. There is no salary attached to either post.

This situation arose because serving in Parliament was often seen in the past as an obligation, rather than an honour. So, an MP who wished to resign had to have an acceptable reason that would disqualify them from continuing in Parliament. One way of doing this was to hold a paid office of the Crown. This convention continues today as a device allowing an MP to leave Parliament other than at an election.

Standards

MPs may not be paid for speaking or asking questions in the House of Commons on behalf of someone who is not an MP. MPs are able to have other paid jobs if they wish. They must declare these and any other matters that might be thought to influence their views.

Parliament

 Elections

General elections

A general election takes place when people throughout the country vote to elect their MP. On such an occasion all seats in the House of Commons are up for election.

The UK is divided into 646 areas, known as constituencies, each of which elects one person to sit as Member of Parliament (MP) for that constituency. Each elector can cast one vote and the person with the most votes in the constituency becomes MP.

The *Parliament Act 1911* states that a general election must be held at least every five years.

Wartime measures

The life of a Parliament can only be extended if both Houses of Parliament agree. This has happened twice. There were eight years (1910–1918) between elections at the time of the First World War and ten years (1935–1945) at the time of the Second World War.

Who is entitled to vote?

All British, Irish and Commonwealth citizens may vote in elections to the House of Commons providing they are on the electoral register, are 18 or over, and are not disqualified to vote. Irish and Commonwealth citizens must be resident in the UK.

The electoral register

The electoral register is a list of all the people who are eligible to vote and have registered to do so. If you are eligible to vote, you may register at any time by contacting your local council election registration office. Voter registration forms are also available via the Internet from the Electoral Commission, **www.electoralcommission.org.uk**.

The electoral register is also updated annually, and an electoral registration form is sent to all households in September or October each year. The name of anyone in the household who will become 18 before the following February may be added to this. Electoral Registers are available for reference in public libraries and local authority offices.

Certain groups are not permitted to vote. These currently include:
- **members of the House of Lords**
- **convicted prisoners while they are held in prison**
- **anyone convicted of corrupt practices at an election within the last five years**
- **offenders compulsorily held in detention for treatment for mental illness.**

Voting in some countries, such as Australia, Belgium and Italy, is compulsory. In the UK it is not, although it has been suggested recently that compulsory voting would reverse declining turn outs.

The right to vote

The right of all men and women in the UK to vote has existed for less than a century. Before 1832 only about five per cent of the population had the franchise, as it was called, and although reforms in 1867 and 1884 increased this figure, the right to vote was still denied to women. In 1918 all men over 21 and women over 30 became able to vote, and ten years later women were given the vote on the same basis as men. The voting age was lowered to 18 by the *Family Law Reform Act 1969.*

By-elections

A by-election is an election held in just one individual constituency. A by-election will normally be held because of the sitting MP's death or resignation.

Political Parties

Most candidates for Parliament represent one of the three main political parties in Great Britain, or a nationalist party in Scotland or Wales. Different party groups exist in Northern Ireland, who also elect MPs. Independent candidates or those representing smaller parties are rarely elected. In the 2005 election, only three of the 646 MPs elected were not from main or nationalist parties.

Candidates

A candidate for election to Parliament must be over the age of 21 and a British citizen, or a citizen of the Republic of Ireland. There are proposals before Parliament to reduce the age of candidacy to 18.

People not entitled to stand for election include judges, civil servants, members of the armed forces and the police – as well as all those opposite who are not eligible to vote.

Anyone who wishes to stand for election must also have the support of ten other electors and pay a deposit of £500. This is lost if the candidate fails to gain five per cent of the total votes cast in the constituency. A candidate must stand either for a registered political party or as an independent candidate.

Parliament

Voting

Most people cast their vote at a polling station. An official takes their name, checks that it is on the list of eligible voters and gives the voter a ballot paper.

Voting takes place in a booth that is screened so that it is not possible for anyone to see how a person votes. After putting a cross on the ballot paper opposite the name of the candidate or party they wish to vote for, they place the ballot paper in the box beside the official.

Election day

By convention, elections in the UK are normally held on a Thursday, but this is not set out in law. The last occasion when this did not happen was for the general election held on Tuesday 27th October 1931.

In order to achieve as high a turnout as possible, general elections are normally held in the spring or autumn. This is designed to avoid people being prevented from voting through bad weather or by being on holiday.

Postal voting

Since 2000 it has been possible for any elector in England, Wales and Scotland to apply for a postal vote. Until then, this was only available to those registered voters who were unable to be in the constituency on voting day. Ballot papers are sent in advance to those who have applied to vote by post, and these must be returned to their local electoral registration office, together with a signed declaration, on or before polling day.

Voting by proxy

Someone unable to vote in person may choose to have someone vote on their behalf. This can be anyone – provided they are eligible to vote, and willing to do so. Further information is available from local electoral registration offices and **www.aboutmyvote.co.uk**.

Electronic voting

At present it is not possible to vote on-line. Investigations and trials are being carried out to see if various forms of e-voting might be possible in future elections.

Voting systems

Votes for general and by-elections are counted on a 'first-past-the-post' system. Each voter casts one vote for the candidate of their choice, and the winning candidate is the person with most votes.

Elections to the European Parliament, the National Assembly for Wales, the Scottish Parliament, the Northern Ireland Assembly, and the London Assembly use other voting systems. These together are known as proportional representation, as they are designed to make the number of seats won at an election more proportional to the number of votes cast.

The election campaign

Once the Prime Minister has called a general election and Parliament has been dissolved, there cease to be any MPs, and the official election campaign begins. During this time, normally lasting three to six weeks, political parties begin to campaign for votes. Each party produces a manifesto setting out the policies it intends to pursue if elected.

Two hundred years ago, voters had to vote in public, making it possible for anyone to discover who they were supporting. Some were bribed or forced into voting for a particular candidate. There were no limits on how much money could be spent, so it was possible to "buy" votes with cash or gifts. Voters in constituencies with only a small number of registered voters sometimes faced strong pressure to vote for a particular candidate from a local aristocratic family.

Today the law governs the way elections are carried out to ensure that they are conducted fairly and that the results are accurate.

Secrecy
Voting is by secret ballot. Parliament has established strict rules about the procedures to be followed at polling stations to make sure that the election is carried out fairly. In addition to the voters, only certain people are allowed to be present at a polling station.

Spending
Parliament has set limits on how much any candidate or party may spend on election expenses. A candidate who is discovered to have exceeded the amount, or misused the money, may face criminal charges. A candidate who is elected and then found guilty of misusing election expenses will lose their seat.

Parliament

Media coverage

The law attempts to ensure equality and fairness in the media coverage of an election. Official party election broadcasts must be shown on BBC and ITV, who have a legal duty to cover the election impartially. Political advertisements on television are not allowed. Newspapers do not have the same duty to report impartially on an election and may seek to influence their readers.

Boundaries

The boundaries between constituencies are redrawn every eight to ten years to make sure that they are all of roughly equal size. Each of the four countries of the UK has an independent organisation called the Boundary Commission to carry this out. Each constituency has, on average, about 68,000 voters.

Control of Elections

The Electoral Commission was established in 2000 to monitor the ways in which elections are held and political parties operate. One of its most important jobs is to check how parties obtain their funding and what they spend on election campaigns. For further details see **www.electoralcommission.org.uk**.

Little and large

In the 2005 election, the Western Isles of Scotland (officially known by its Gaelic name of Na H-Eileanan an Iar) was the smallest constituency to send an MP to Westminster. It has an electorate of 21,576. The Isle of Wight was the largest with an electorate of 109,046.

After the election

When all the results of the election are known, the queen or king will usually invite the leader of the party winning the most seats in the House of Commons to be Prime Minister and form a government. The second largest party becomes the Official Opposition.

Shortly after the general election newly elected MPs meet at the House of Commons to prepare for the new Parliament. All MPs must swear or affirm their allegiance to the Crown before they are able to take up their seats.

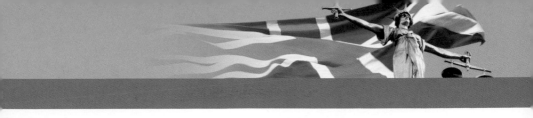

The House of Lords

The House of Lords is the second chamber of the UK Parliament and sometimes known as the upper house. It shares with the House of Commons the role of making law, and debating and examining the actions of the government. Members of the Lords are not elected and are unpaid, although they do receive an attendance allowance.

Many other countries have two 'chambers' or 'houses'. The advantage of this is felt to be to provide a place for reflection and second thoughts on new legislation, particularly if the government has a large majority in the lower house or the matter has not been extensively debated.

Making law

The House of Lords' scrutiny of legislation is an important part of the law-making process and it spends about two thirds of its time in discussing proposals for new law. There is broad acceptance in the upper house that, as MPs are elected and Lords are not, debates on the principles of legislation should be resolved in the House of Commons. Generally therefore the House of Lords acts as a revising chamber, altering details of Bills.

Changes

The Lords can suggest changes to almost all legislation – except those dealing directly with public money and taxation. Another restriction – although unwritten – is that the House of Lords may not block measures that have been contained in a governing party's election manifesto, see page 129.

Normally the agreement of the House of Lords is needed for any Bill to become law, but this is not always the case. If the House of Lords refuses to support a Bill that has been passed by the House of Commons, the *Parliament Act* may be used to solve the dispute.

The Parliament Acts

Until the early twentieth century the House of Lords had the power to block legislation introduced by the government. This power was removed by the *Parliament Acts 1911* and *1949* which allow the House of Commons to pass a Bill into law without the Lords' agreement after a delay of one year.

The House of Lords rarely tries to block legislation completely. Since 1949 only four Acts have passed into law without the consent of the House of Lords. The *Hunting Act 2004* is the most recent example of this.

Parliament

Hereditary peers

Hereditary peers inherit their title through their family. Until 1999, the House included over 700 peers who had inherited their titles. The *House of Lords Act 1999* removed the right of many of these peers to sit and vote in the House of Lords. There are now 92 seats for hereditary peers in the Lords of which 17 are reserved for various office holders. The remaining 75 are elected from within their number by the hereditary peers.

Life peers

Until 1958, the House of Lords was entirely made up of hereditary peers. Life peers are appointed by the Queen on the advice of the Prime Minister. By convention a certain number can be proposed by the Leader of the Opposition and other party leaders. Life peers cannot pass their title onto their children or other members of their family.

Many life peerages are granted to former MPs and other supporters as a reward for political service and loyalty. Life peerages are also awarded to people who have shown outstanding ability in their field, for example in science and industry, entertainment and the arts, education or medicine.

Membership

Unlike the House of Commons, there is no fixed number of members of the House of Lords. Although members are organised on party lines in much the same way as the House of Commons, there are important differences in that Lords do not represent a constituency and many are not members of any political party. There is a general agreement that no party should have a majority in the House of Lords.

There are 725 members of the House of Lords (March 2006). Most of these are life peers, but some are hereditary peers. Senior churchmen (Lords Spiritual) and judges (Law Lords) are also members of the House of Lords.

Details of the membership of the House of Lords and party strength are available from the UK Parliament website **www.parliament.uk**.

People's peers

Since 2000, it has been possible for members of the public to nominate someone (or themselves) for a life peerage. Applications are made to the House of Lords Appointments Commission, which has the job of checking nominations, interviewing those whom it feels might be suitable and then passing the names of those people it believes should become life peers to the Prime Minister.

Twenty-nine people have now become life peers in this way. Most have been people already well-known in public life.

Bishops and judges

The Church of England is the official, or established, Church in England, and because of this, its 26 most senior bishops are entitled to sit in the House of Lords. They are known as the Lords Spiritual.

The House of Lords has had an important role as the final Court of Appeal in the UK justice system, see page 140. The twelve senior judges who carry out this role are known as Lords of Appeal in Ordinary and, in order to do this, are appointed life peers. They may speak and vote on all the business of the House of Lords, but in practice rarely do so. Nor do they usually become involved in any matter of party political controversy.

Crossbenchers

Members of the government and opposition parties in the House of Lords sit on benches in the chamber facing one another. By tradition, those peers who are independent and not representatives of a political party sit on the benches situated in the middle of the chamber. These are known as crossbenchers – peers who sit on benches that cross the chamber of the House of Lords.

Reforming the House of Lords

Over the years, the unelected nature of the House of Lords has been the subject of controversy. As early as 1886, a debate took place in the House of Commons on the wisdom of having a legislative system that was at least partly controlled by heredity. During the twentieth century various changes took place that reduced the power of the House of Lords, and broadened its membership, see **Life peers**.

In 1999 most of the 750 hereditary peers lost their right to sit and vote in the House of Lords. This was intended to be the first stage of a two-stage process. However, there has since been no agreement on how to take the reform forward. This is largely because of disagreement over whether the Lords should contain elected members and, if so, in what proportion. The Labour government elected in 2005 promised MPs a free vote on the composition of the House of Lords. (In a free vote, MPs can vote as they wish, and are not controlled by their party's policy.

Law, courts & judges

CONDUCTED ACCORDING TO LAW

Judges and courts have a very important constitutional role in upholding the law and protecting people's rights and freedoms. The separation of the judiciary (the system of courts and judges) from government is felt to be an important part of this.

An independent system of judges and courts helps to make sure that the law is applied equally to everyone and that no one (not even the government) is above the law.

A just society also needs rules and procedures that protect people from injustice. Trials and hearings in court should be fair. This means, for example, that both sides in a dispute have the opportunity to present their side of the argument; people should not be punished, unless they have broken the law; and a person should not be a judge in his or her own case.

The right to a fair trial, contained in Article 6 of the European Convention on Human Rights, is incorporated into UK law by the *Human Rights Act 1998.*

The European Convention on Human Rights, Article 6

" … everyone is entitled to a fair and public hearing within a reasonable time by an independent and impartial tribunal established by law. Judgement shall be pronounced publicly …

"Everyone charged with a criminal offence shall be presumed innocent until proved guilty according to law."

Law

The legal system in Britain

Britain has three separate legal systems – those of England and Wales, Scotland, and Northern Ireland.

The basis of the legal system in Scotland is different from the rest of the UK. This is because it had its own system of law, based in Edinburgh, before union with England in 1707. There are a number of significant differences between law in Scotland and England and Wales.

Northern Ireland's legal system is similar to that of England and Wales, although one notable feature is that juries are not used for terrorist trials.

This chapter is concerned with the system as it operates in England and Wales.

Making the law

There are three major sources of law in Britain: common law, statute law and European law.

Common law

When William the Conqueror invaded England in 1066, no system of justice covered the whole country. In the years that followed, in an attempt to create a central system of justice, the King and those he appointed as judges would travel the country listening to disputes and then give judgement. In making these judgements the King's judges gradually formed a set of laws that were common to the whole country.

Common law is based on precedent – that is, decisions reached in other similar cases. This ensures that similar cases are dealt with in a consistent way. However there are times when the circumstances of a case have not arisen before, or when senior judges decide that existing judgements do not reflect modern society. In these situations, by their decision, the most senior judges can create or change the law. Common law has developed over time and is based on decisions made by the courts.

Changing times

In 1992, five senior judges had to decide whether a man could be found guilty of raping his wife. As the law stood at the time, this was not possible. Under common law it was assumed that, by getting married, a woman automatically gave her consent to her husband for sexual intercourse.

The judges decided that this rule (which went back to before 1736) should no longer be part of the law, since husbands and wives today are seen as equal partners in marriage. The decision of the judges changed the law, and as a result a man who forces his wife to have sex against her will is now guilty of rape.

Although judge-made law is still important, most of our law today comes from Parliament.

Law, courts & judges

Statute law

Statute law is made by an Act of Parliament. As Britain became a more industrial and urban society in the nineteenth century, there was a clear need for new laws and regulations. The system of common law that had existed for centuries could not cope with these new circumstances. As a result, statute law became much more important and today is the major source of new law.

European law

The UK's membership of the European Union requires all our laws to follow the treaties and agreements that we have made as members of the EU. British courts are bound by decisions made by the European Court of Justice and the European Court of Human Rights, see pages 107 and 110.

Courts

Courts are places set up for the administration of justice. They carry out a number of functions. These include:

- **settling disputes between individuals, companies, or public bodies**
- **dealing with issues relating to children and other family matters**
- **hearing criminal trials – deciding on the innocence or guilt of the accused**
- **sentencing the guilty.**

There are many different kinds of courts and tribunals, and three distinct systems within the UK for England and Wales, Scotland and Northern Ireland. Details of the court structures in each of these areas are available from court service websites: **www.hmcourts-service.gov.uk** (England and Wales), **www.courtsni.gov.uk** (Northern Ireland), and **www.scotcourts.gov.uk** (Scotland).

Sometimes cases in court are decided by a judge alone, others by more than one judge or magistrate, or with a jury. Members of the public are admitted into some courts and tribunals, other are held behind closed doors.

Magistrates' courts

The vast majority of criminal cases are dealt with in magistrates' courts by magistrates or Justices of the Peace (JPs), as they are also known. There are magistrates' courts in towns and cities throughout England and Wales. Magistrates are drawn from members of the local community. They are not legal specialists, but are given training for the job. Magistrates work unpaid.

Magistrates also deal with cases involving young people, children and parents, and other matters, such as licensing.

County courts

The county court system was set up just over a hundred years ago to provide a relatively cheap way for people to settle disputes. They still operate in the same way today, with judges usually sitting alone, handling a wide range of civil law cases, including debt, breach of contract, housing matters, divorce and adoption.

Tribunals

Although not strictly courts, tribunals can provide a relatively quick and informal way of settling disputes. They cover many areas of life and are now used by more people than the civil courts. Areas covered include: employment rights, tax, immigration, parking, mental health, school admissions and special needs.

Cases are heard by a panel of three people, a legally qualified chairperson and two people qualified in the area concerned. Members of the public should be able to take their case to a tribunal relatively easily and cheaply. Hearings should be held in public, with the panel clearly explaining the reasons for its decision. More information is available on the Tribunals Service website, **www.tribunals.gov.uk**.

Law, courts & judges

Criminal and civil law

There are several different ways to classify law. One of the most commonly used is criminal and civil law.

Criminal law covers wrongdoings that Parliament and courts consider so serious as to be called "offences" and for which people are tried and punished by the state. Criminal law covers a wide range of activities from murder and theft, to flying a kite near an airfield.

Civil law deals with legal matters between individuals, organisations or companies and between the individual and the state that are not covered by criminal law. Civil law covers many areas of life including business, employment, housing and family matters. Civil law cases often lead to compensation for the injured party (such as a person who has been unfairly dismissed from work) or to an order requiring someone to behave in a particular way.

The Crown Court

The Crown Court deals with serious criminal cases such as murder and robbery. There are courts in most large towns and cities throughout England and Wales.

If the defendant pleads not guilty the case is heard by a judge and jury. If the defendant pleads or is found guilty, sentence is passed by a judge.

Juries

The use of juries in criminal trials in England and Wales goes back more than 800 years. Although the ways in which juries operate have changed greatly during this time they have always been based on the idea of using ordinary local people in the administration of justice.

Jury trials have not always been satisfactory. In the past, judges would pressurise juries to come to a particular decision, even refusing them food and water until they reached agreement.

Today people are selected for jury service by having their name drawn at random from the local register of electors. A jury is made up of 12 people (15 in Scotland) aged between 18 and 70. Almost anyone may be called for jury service, although people on bail or probation and those who have served a custodial sentence in the last ten years are ineligible. Jury service is compulsory; failure to attend may result in a fine.

In recent years, the government has proposed not using juries for less serious cases and in complex fraud trials. This has been controversial. One of the main arguments put forward in favour of juries is that using ordinary people to decide the innocence or guilt of the accused creates greater public involvement and confidence in the system of justice. Juries also may act as guardians against what they believe to be unfairness or oppression.

Not guilty

In January 1996, three women walked into a hangar at a British Aerospace factory in Lancashire. With household hammers they caused £1.5m damage to a jet fighter that was due to be delivered to Indonesia – whose government at the time was persecuting thousands of people in nearby East Timor.

Before leaving the factory, the women told security staff what they had done, claiming that they had not committed a crime, but performed a duty. They were charged with criminal damage, and sent for trial in court. Despite overwhelming evidence, the jury acquitted all three women.

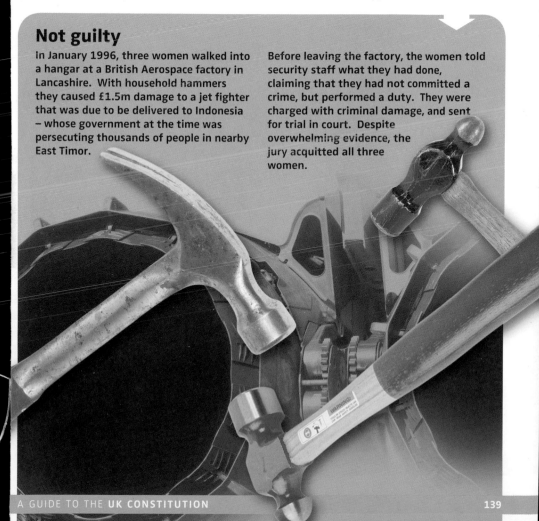

Law, courts & judges

The High Court of Justice

This is the main civil court in England and Wales, where the most serious cases are heard. The High Court is divided into separate divisions specialising in different kinds of cases such as company law and taxation, family matters, and personal injury. Cases of people seeking damages after a serious accident will commonly be heard in the High Court.

The Court of Appeal

A person who is unhappy about a decision made by a judge in their case has the right to appeal against this in a higher court. There must be proper grounds for making the appeal, and there are time limits within which it must take place.

Appeals against the decision of a magistrates' court are heard in the Crown Court. Appeals against decisions in Crown or county courts, or the High Court are heard in the Court of Appeal.

The House of Lords

The House of Lords is the most senior court. It acts as the final court on points of law in civil cases for the whole of the UK, and in criminal cases for England, Wales and Northern Ireland.

There are 12 Law Lords, who are all very senior judges, and each case is usually heard by a panel of five.

The Judicial Committee of the Privy Council is the final appeal court for decisions made by courts in some Commonwealth countries, see page 112. The Privy Council also deals with other cases, including those concerning the disqualification of MPs.

The Supreme Court
In 2009, the Supreme Court is expected to come into operation, and will replace the House of Lords as the UK's highest court.

Judges

Judges preside over proceedings in court. This involves ensuring that a case is properly managed, explaining the law to the jury (in criminal cases), giving judgement and, if appropriate, passing sentence.

Applying and interpreting the law

When judges apply the law they interpret the words of an Act of Parliament according to their plain and ordinary meaning. If this leads to an absurd or unfair result, it is Parliament's task to pass a new law to correct the position. It is not the job of a judge to make the law by giving new meanings to the words used.

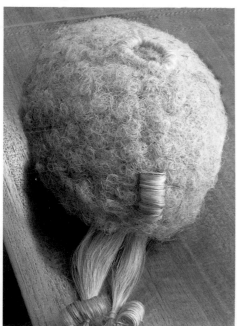

Letter of the law

Mrs Berryman's husband was killed while oiling points along a railway line. She tried to obtain compensation for his death from the railway company. At the time the law stated that compensation in these circumstances was payable only if the line was being "relayed or repaired". The Law Lords decided that oiling the points was maintaining the line, and not "relaying or repairing" it. Mrs Berryman lost her case.

Law, courts & judges

Independence

One of the most important requirements for judges is that they have no connection with the case that they are hearing. They must conduct the case in a fair and balanced way, and the judgement they give must be completely impartial. Judges must not let their personal feelings get in the way of how they apply the law, nor should they allow anyone or anything to influence their decision.

In the interest of justice

In 1998, General Pinochet, former Chilean Head of State, visited England. Whilst he was staying in London a warrant was issued in Spain for the General's arrest. The Spanish authorities were investigating the torture and disappearance of a number of Spanish citizens in Chile during General Pinochet's time in power, and wanted to question him about his involvement in this.

The General was arrested and held in Britain, but the legality of this was challenged by his lawyers who claimed that, as a former head of state he could not be arrested and tried in another country for the things that he had done when in office.

Five Law Lords sat in judgement of this case. One was Lord Hoffmann, who was also a director of Amnesty International, the human rights organisation. Amnesty International had a strong interest in the case and was one of the groups supporting General Pinochet's arrest.

Lord Hoffmann, however, had failed to disclose his interest in the case and was, as one Law Lord said, "a judge in his own cause". Although there was no suggestion that Lord Hoffman was deliberately biased, the Law Lords decided that the case would have to be heard all over again – but without Lord Hoffmann.

The outcome in the second hearing was the same as the first, with the judges deciding that General Pinochet could be taken from Britain to face charges in Spain. (However, the Home Secretary decided, as was his right, to return General Pinochet to Chile, because of the former head of state's poor health.)

This principle is also established under the Human Rights Act 1998, which incorporates Article 6 of the European Convention on Human Rights, guaranteeing a fair and public hearing "by an independent and impartial tribunal".

Free from government influence

Judges also need to be independent from government. This helps to ensure that cases are dealt with fairly and also gives people protection when the state goes beyond its lawful authority. The independence of the judiciary is underlined in the *Constitutional Reform Act 2005*, which places ministers under a duty to uphold this and not to seek to influence judicial decisions.

The separation of the judiciary from government is maintained in a number of further ways.

Salaries In order to protect judges from a cut in pay if they make a decision that is unpopular with the government, judges are paid from a fund controlled by Parliament, not government.

Security Judges cannot lose their job if they are unpopular with the government, they can only be removed if it is shown that they are in some way unfit to do the job. This could be through a serious disability or misbehaviour, which makes them unsuitable to be a judge. Under the *Act of Settlement 1701*, a senior judge may be dismissed only after a request from both Houses of Parliament to the king or queen.

Junior judges may be removed by the Lord Chancellor with the agreement of the Lord Chief Justice. Although several judges have been convicted of drink-driving offences, this power has only been used once. In 1983 a judge lost his position after being convicted of smuggling whisky and cigarettes into Britain in his yacht.

Appointment To become a judge, it is normally necessary to have worked for a number of years as a barrister or solicitor.

Until recently, the Lord Chancellor has chosen judges after collecting information about possible candidates. Now there is an independent organisation – the Commission for Judicial Appointments – that selects candidates for appointment as senior judges. Once approved, it is the Queen, on the recommendation of the Prime Minister or Lord Chancellor, who formally appoints senior judges. More junior judges are appointed directly by the Lord Chancellor.

Other work Full-time judges may not practice as lawyers, nor may they do other paid work. They are also disqualified from membership of the House of Commons.

Criticism The independence of judges is further protected through convention which dictates that they should not be publicly criticised by members of the government.

Too far

Home Secretary David Blunkett was criticised for undermining the rule of law when, commenting on the case of a sex offender whom he felt had been given too light a sentence, said that people would think that judges "had lost their marbles".

Law, courts & judges

The Lord Chancellor

The office of Lord Chancellor is one of the oldest in the country, dating back to at least 1068, shortly after the Norman Conquest.

Appointed by the Prime Minister, the post used to combine a number of roles. Until 2006, the Lord Chancellor was:

- **a senior member of the government, with a seat in the Cabinet**
- **the Speaker in the House of Lords**
- **the most senior judge in the court structure and head of the judiciary in England and Wales.**

As head of the judiciary (and as Speaker in the House of Lords), the Lord Chancellor was required to be completely impartial. However, many people argued that this was not consistent with the Lord Chancellor's political position as a member of the government.

This situation has been changed by the *Constitutional Reform Act 2005*. In April 2006, the Lord Chancellor's role as head of the judiciary was taken over by the Lord Chief Justice of England and Wales. This person is independent from government and has the job of representing the views of judges in England and Wales to Parliament, the Lord Chancellor and to ministers. As of July 2006, the Lord Chancellor is no longer the Speaker in the House of Lords.

Preventing an abuse of power

The government and public bodies are required to keep to the law in everything they do. If a person feels that they have failed to do this, then the minister or department concerned can be challenged through the courts.

Judicial review

The special procedure though which courts 'review' these decisions is known as judicial review. It involves a judge, or judges examining whether a public body, such as a government department or a local authority, has acted lawfully.

Judicial review looks at how the decision was made. It does not examine whether the decision itself was correct, but whether the public body had the right in law to act as it did.

The review will not substitute what it thinks is the 'correct' decision, though it can set aside a decision which it thinks is unreasonable.

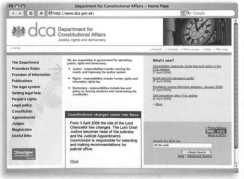

Longer sentence

In 1993, two boys aged 10 and 11, were convicted of the kidnap and murder of three-year-old Jamie Bulger. The judge sentenced the boys to a period of detention of ten years. However, following a public outcry, the Home Secretary increased this to fifteen years.

An appeal was lodged against the Home Secretary's decision, and a judicial review was held. The point at issue was not whether the two boys should serve ten or fifteen years in prison, but whether the Home Secretary had the right, as a government minister, to extend the sentence handed down by the court.

The case was heard at the highest level, in the House of Lords, where it was ruled that the Home Secretary did not have this right, and his decision was overturned.

Claims for judicial review may normally be brought only when all other avenues of complaint have been exhausted, and cases must normally be brought within three months of the event.

INDEX